AF454103

The
Big Book of
Minimal
Tattoos

550 Bohemian Tattoo Designs

Martina Kohls

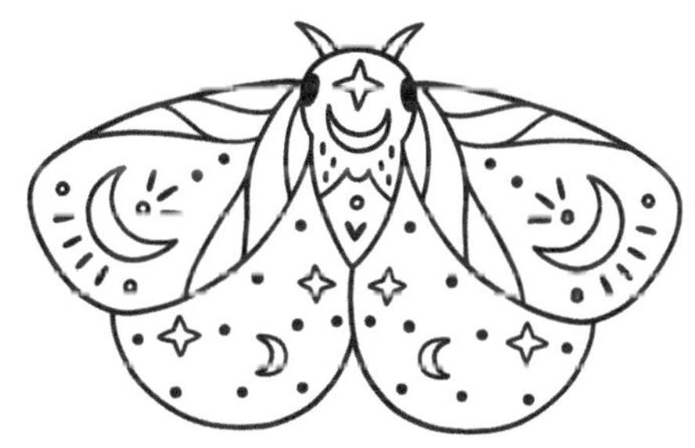

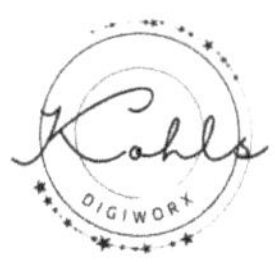

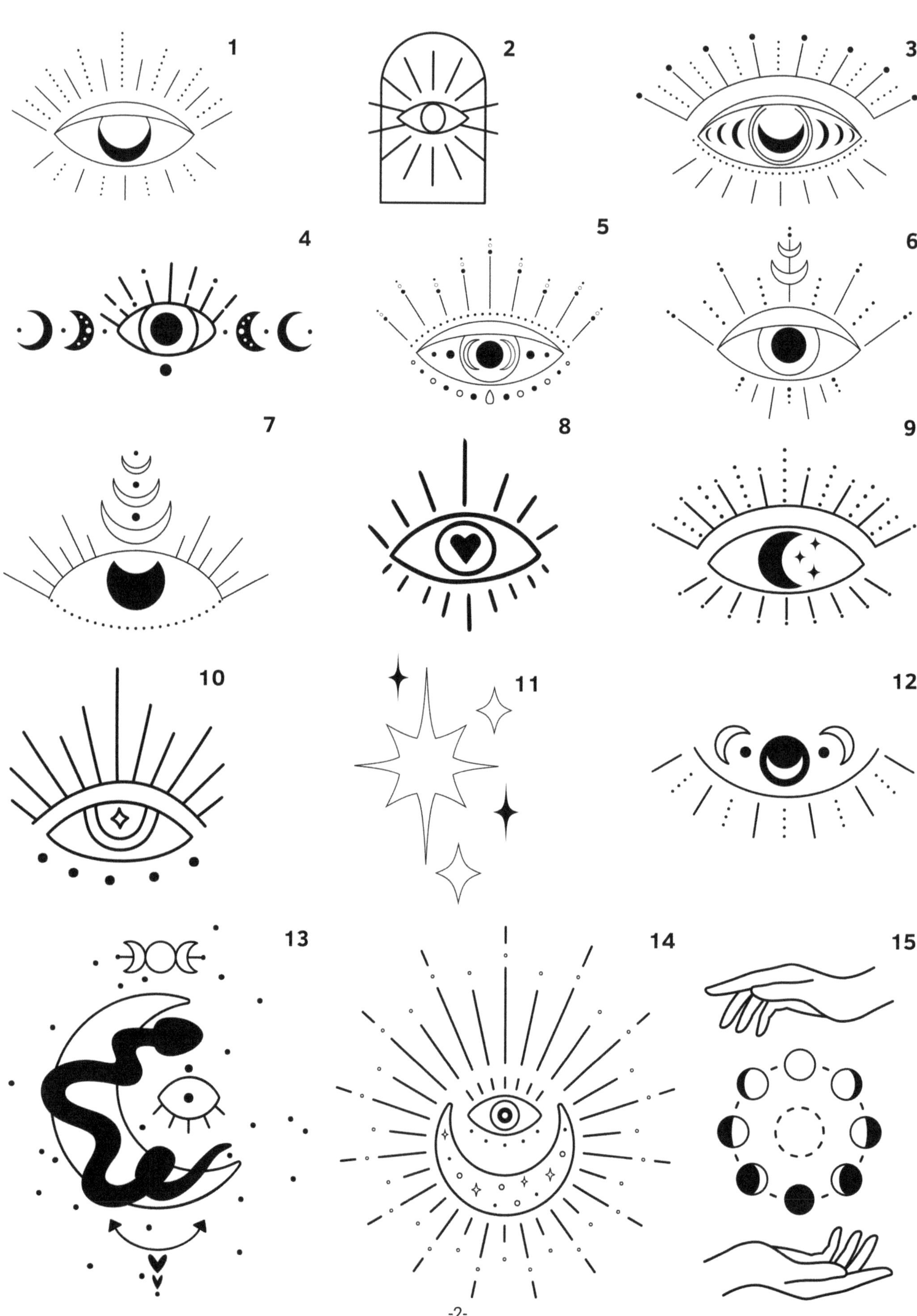

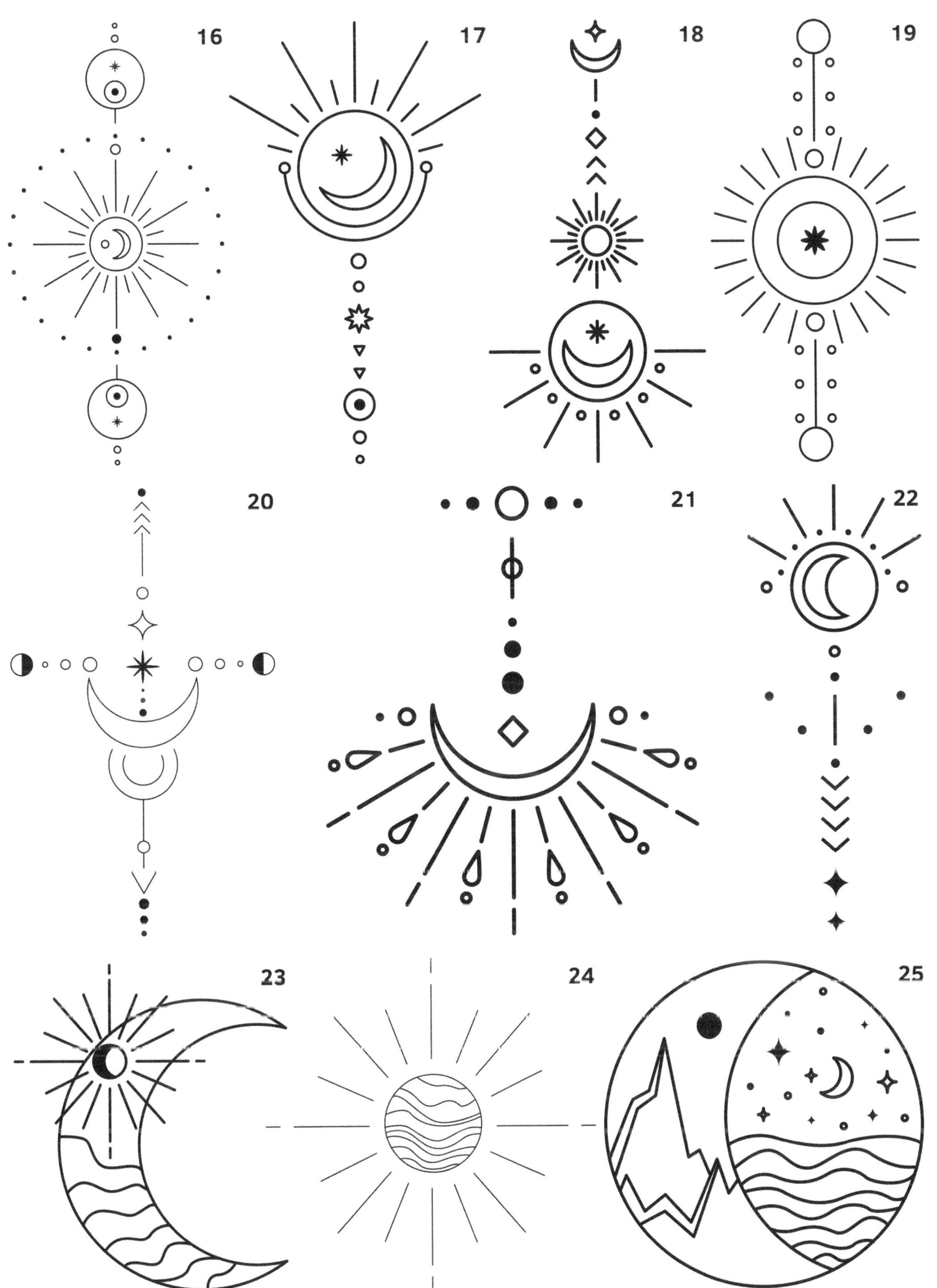

16
17
18
19
20
21
22
23
24
25

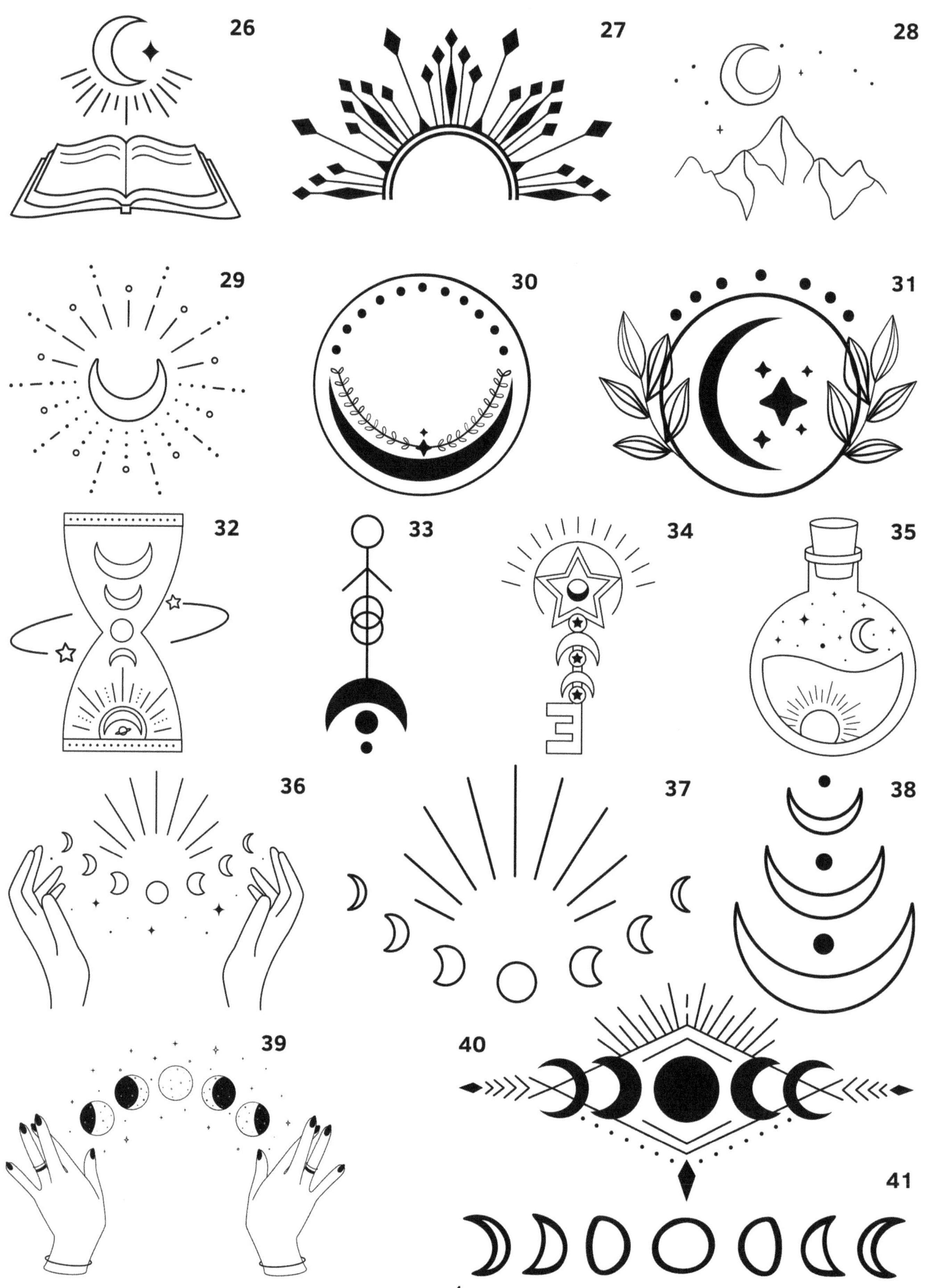

26
27
28
29
30
31
32
33
34
35
36
37
38
39
40
41

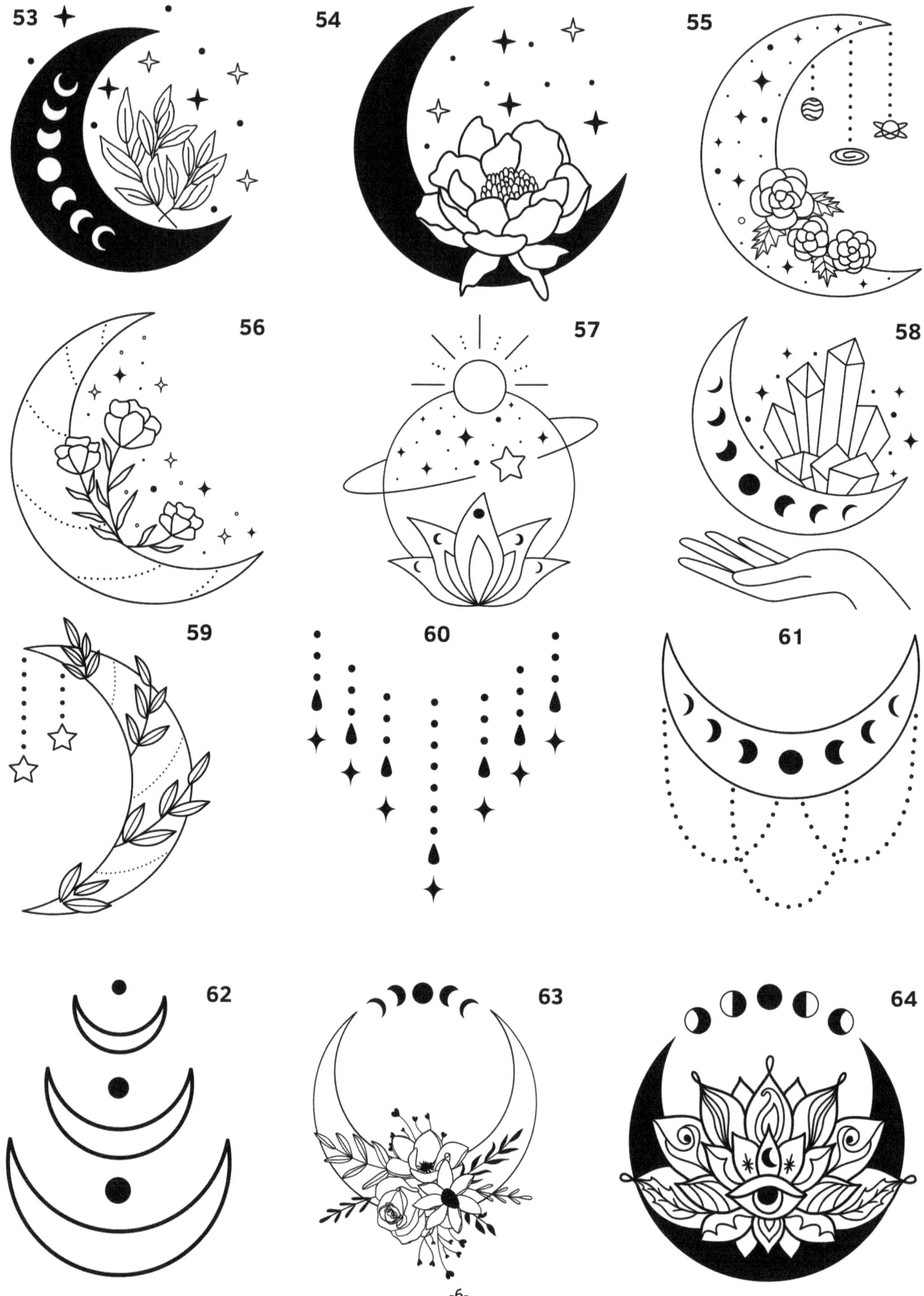

53
54
55
56
57
58
59
60
61
62
63
64

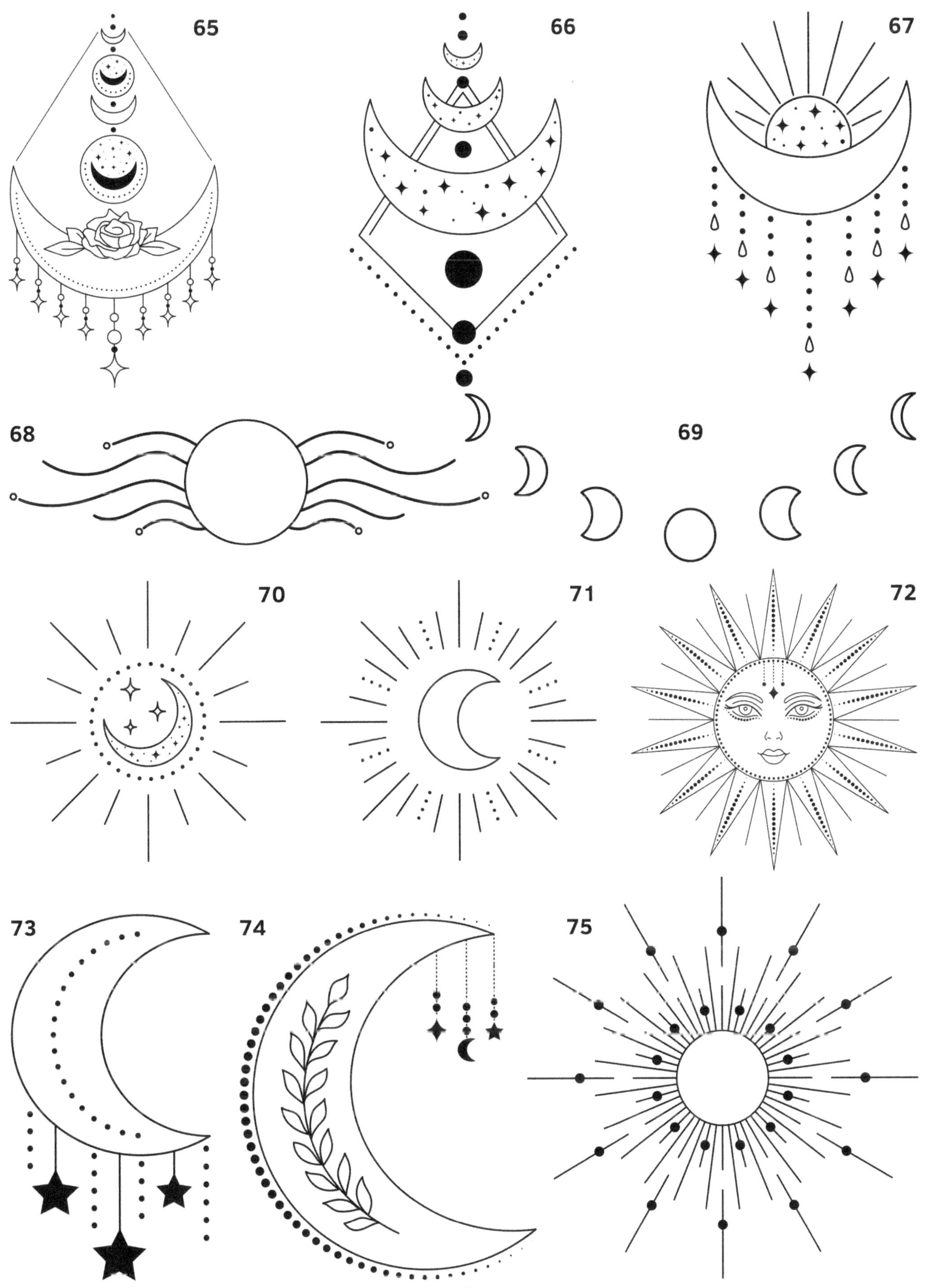

65
66
67
68
69
70
71
72
73
74
75

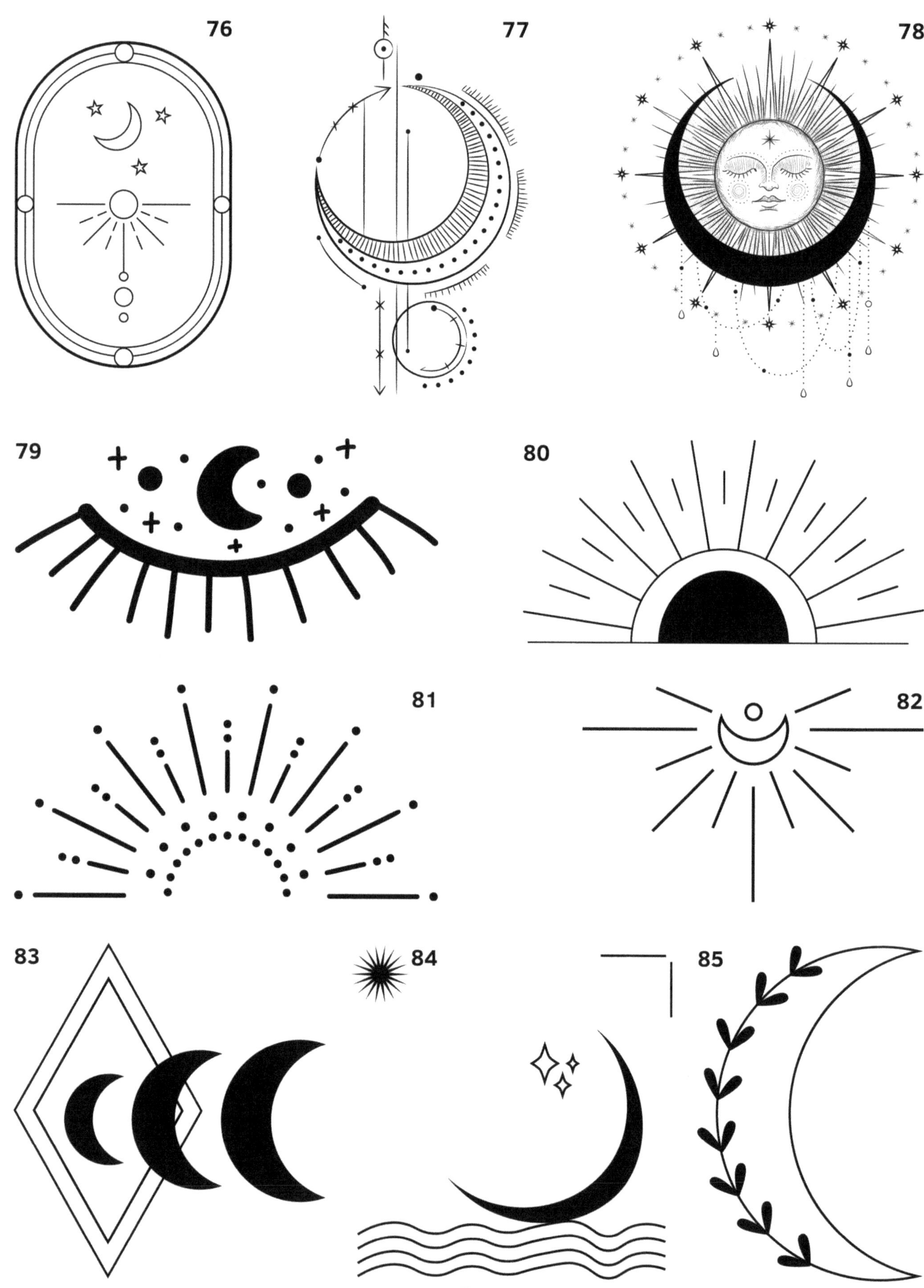

76
77
78
79
80
81
82
83
84
85

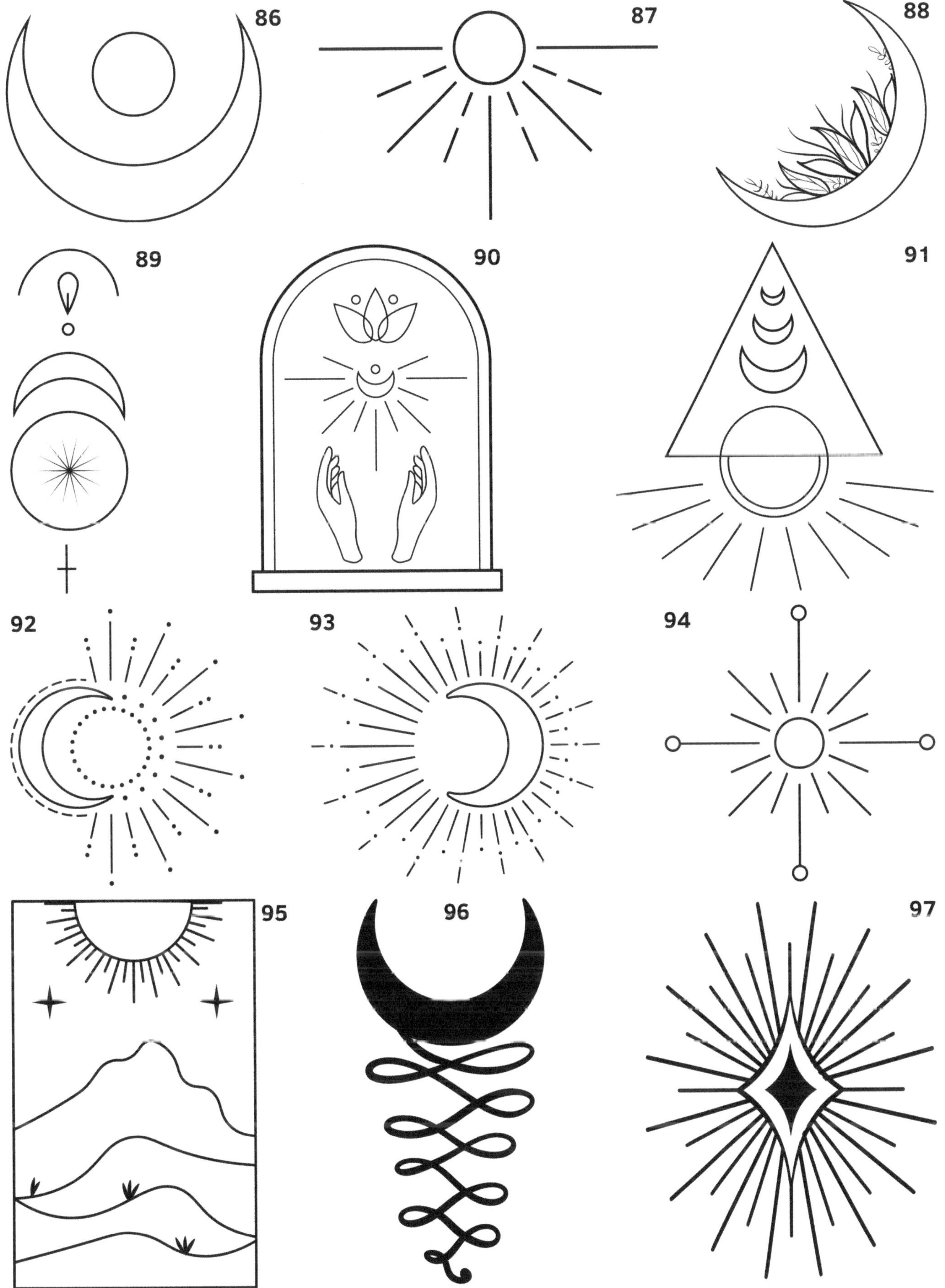

86
87
88
89
90
91
92
93
94
95
96
97

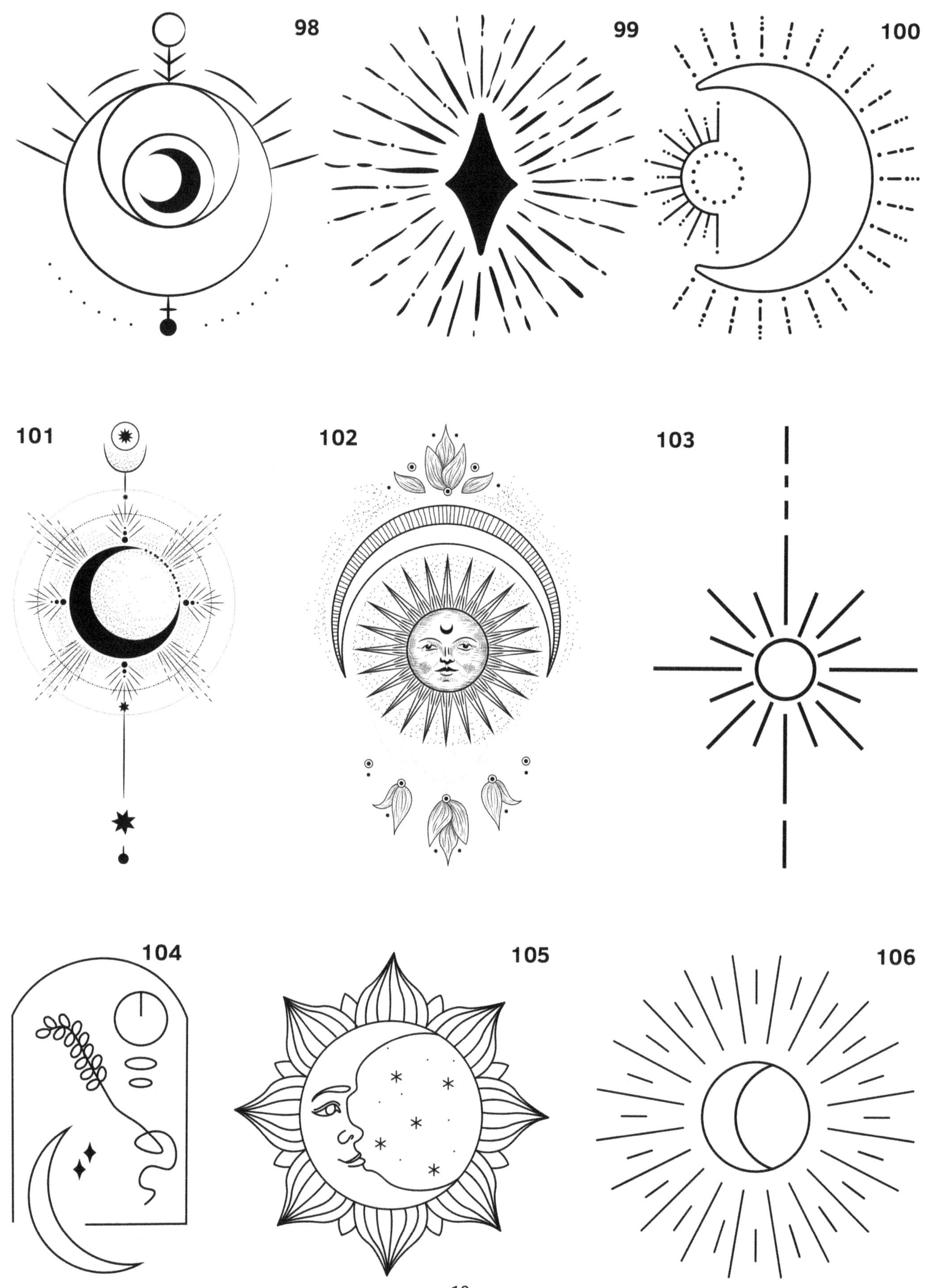

98
99
100
101
102
103
104
105
106

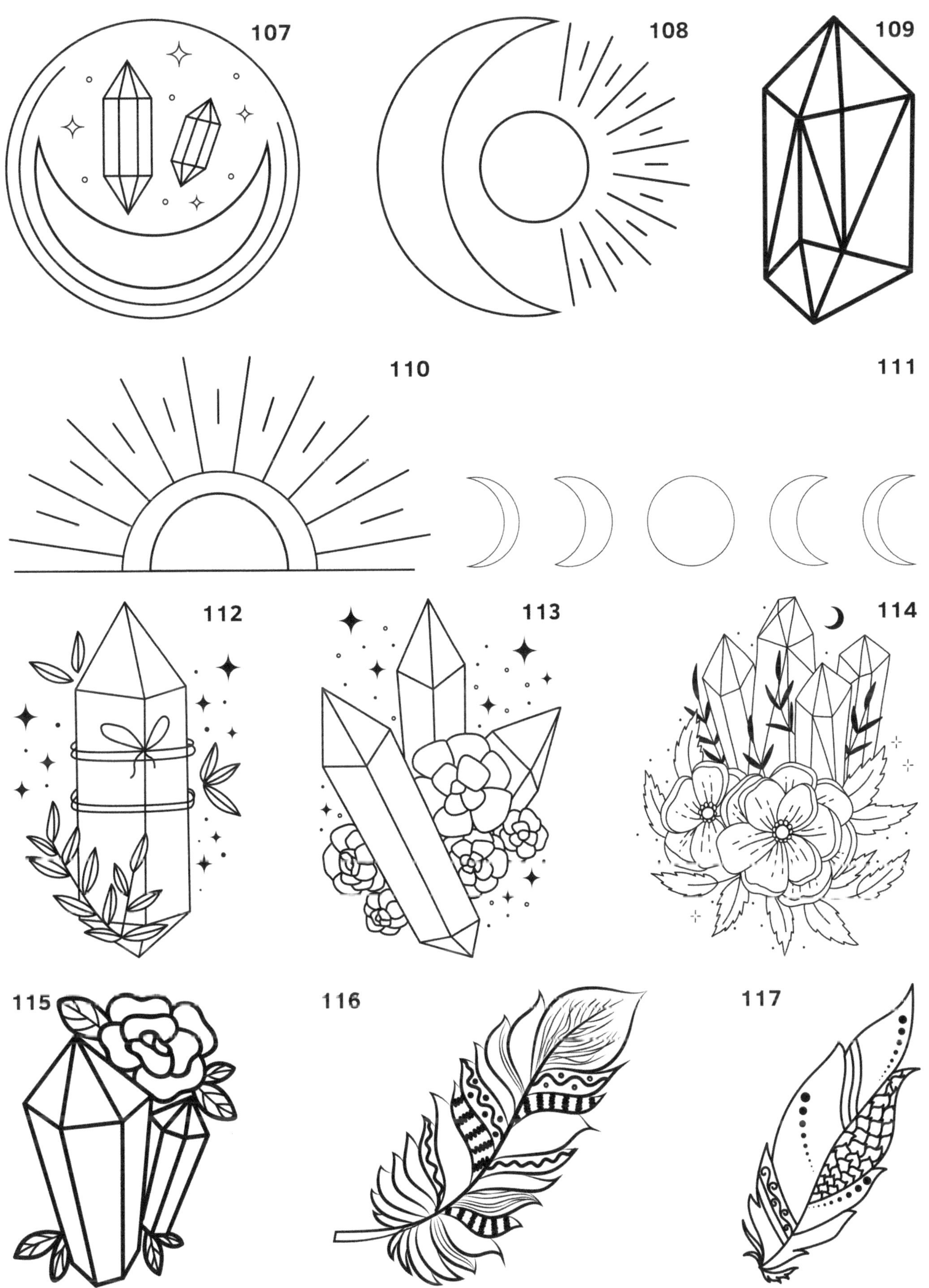
107
108
109
110
111
112
113
114
115
116
117

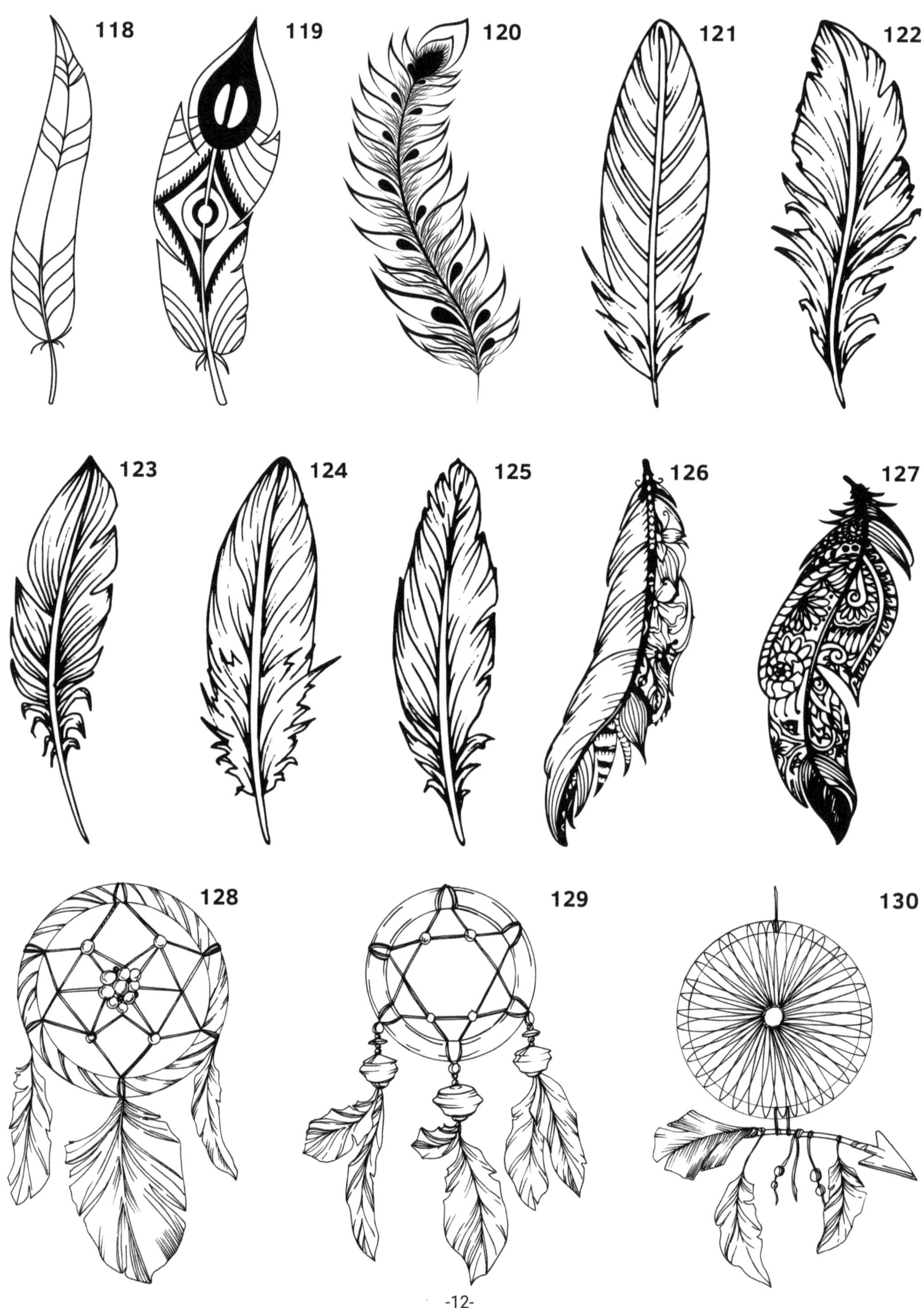

118
119
120
121
122
123
124
125
126
127
128
129
130

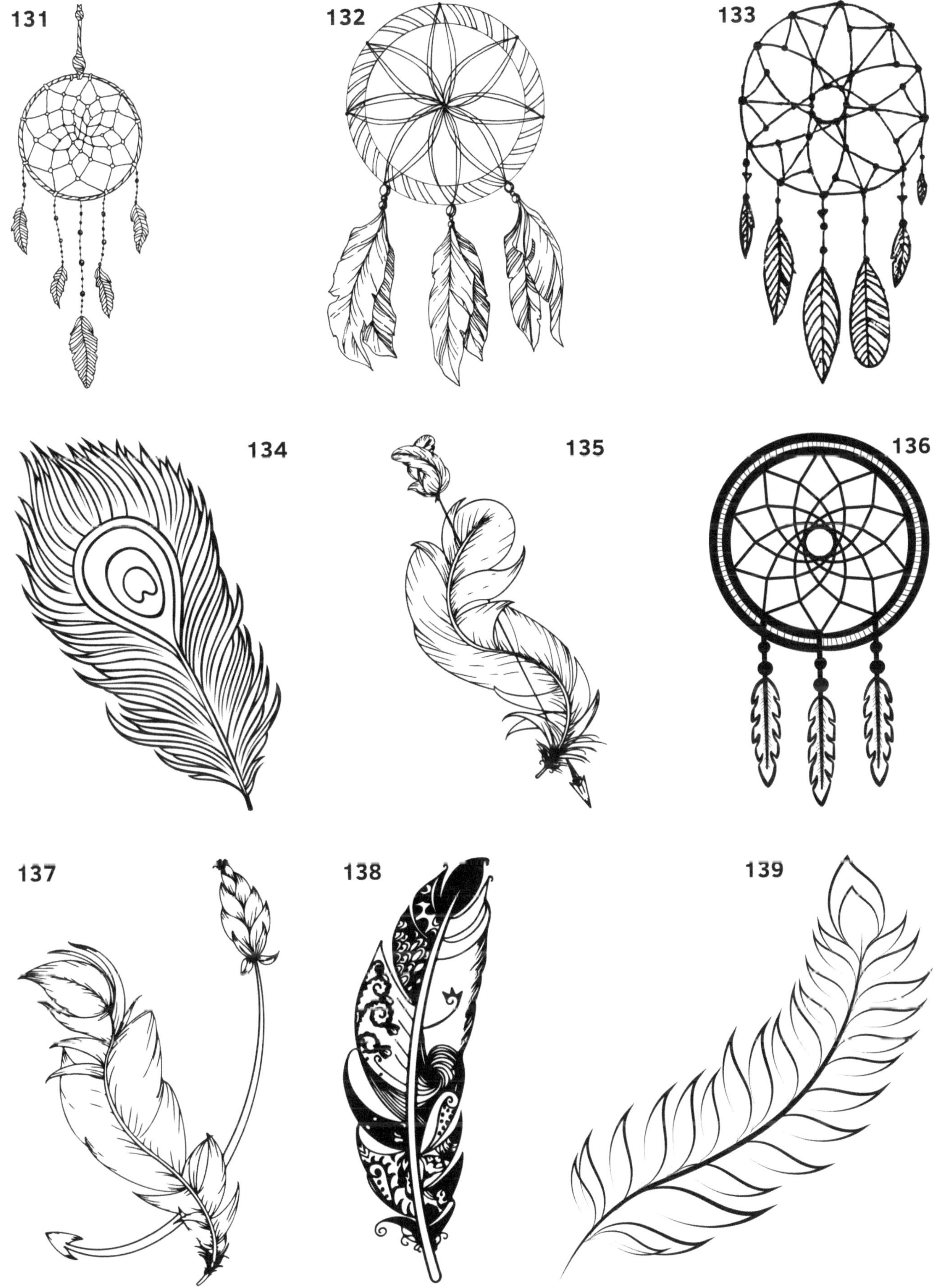

131
132
133
134
135
136
137
138
139

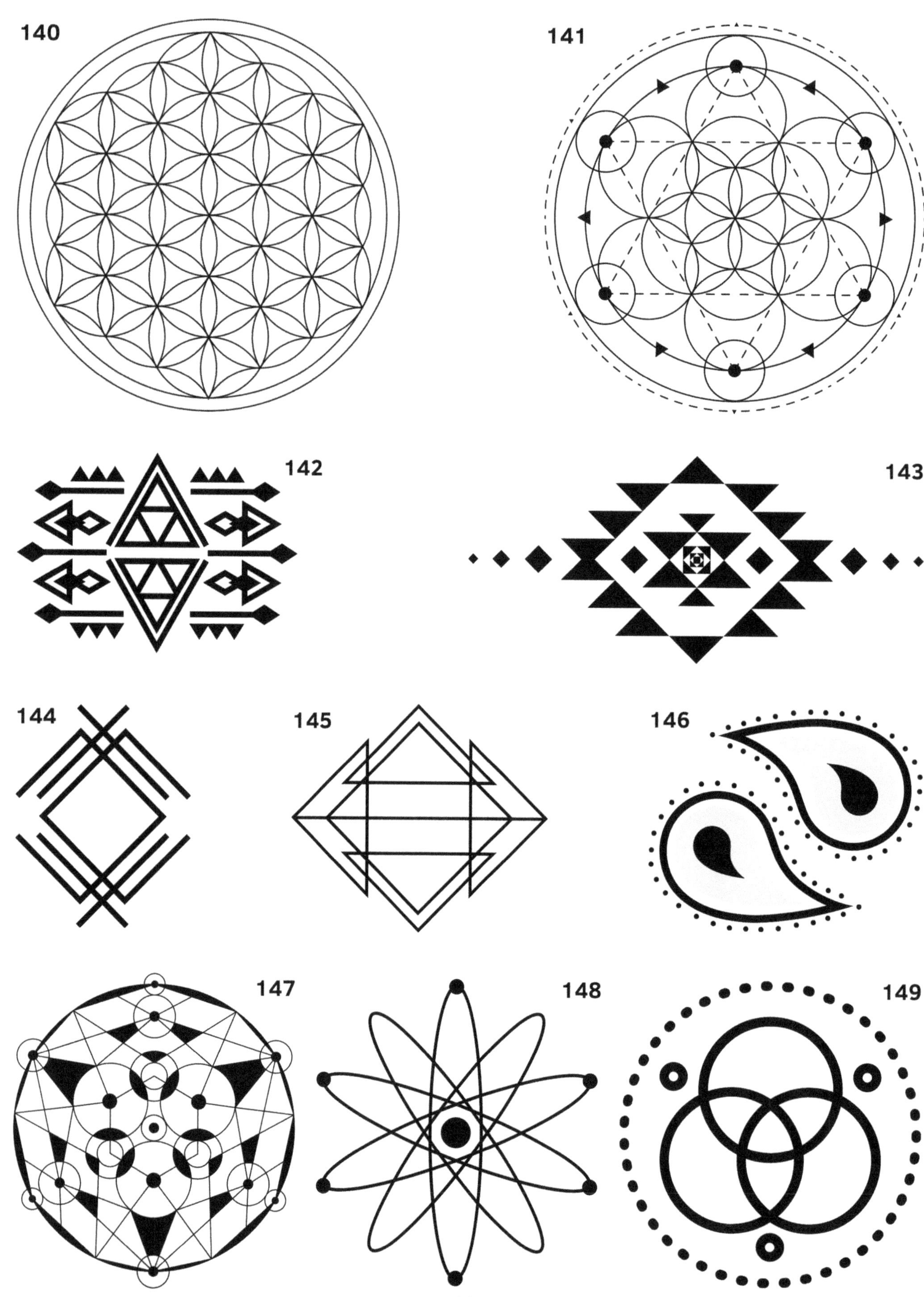

140
141
142
143
144
145
146
147
148
149

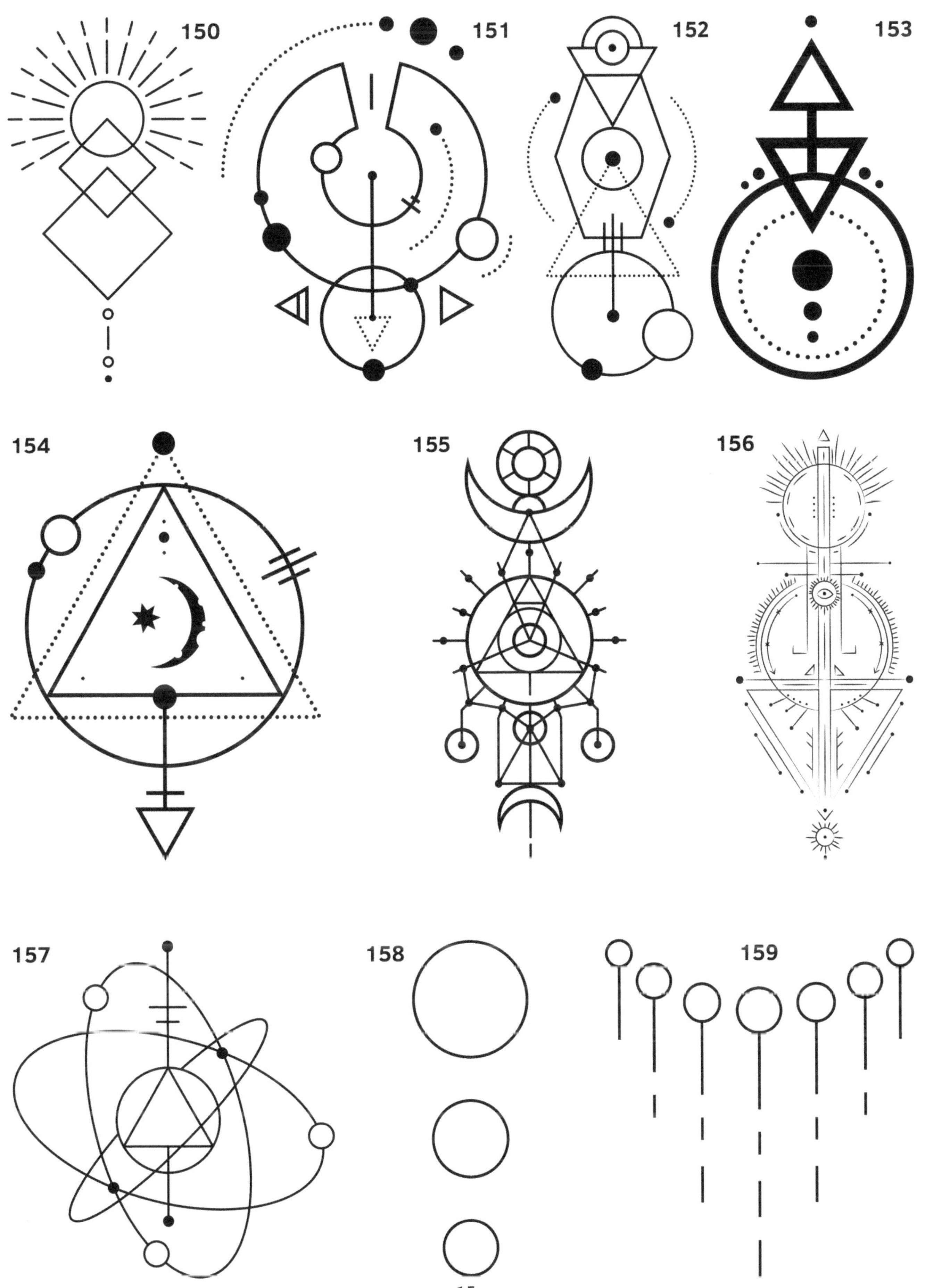

150
151
152
153
154
155
156
157
158
159

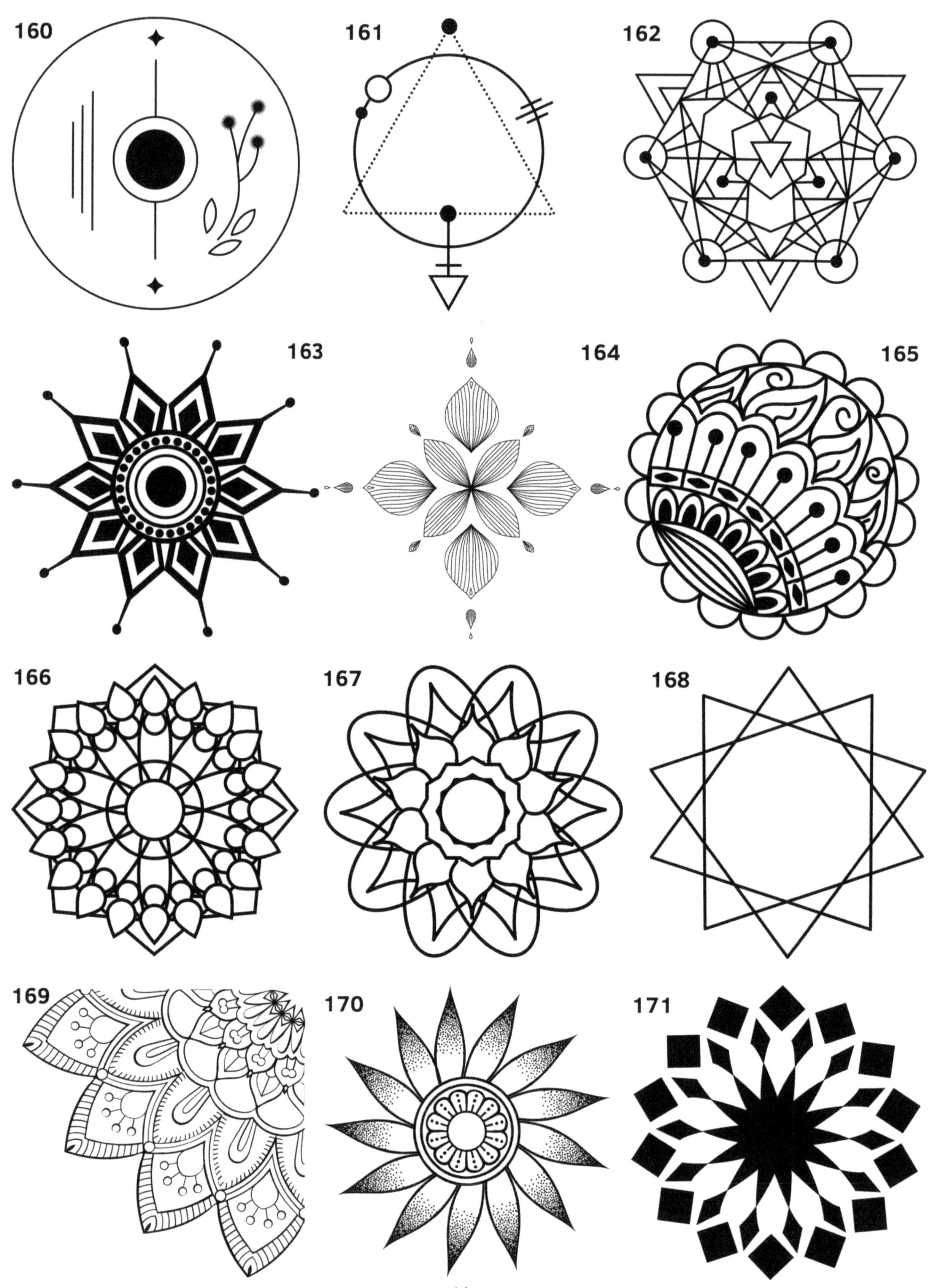
160
161
162
163
164
165
166
167
168
169
170
171

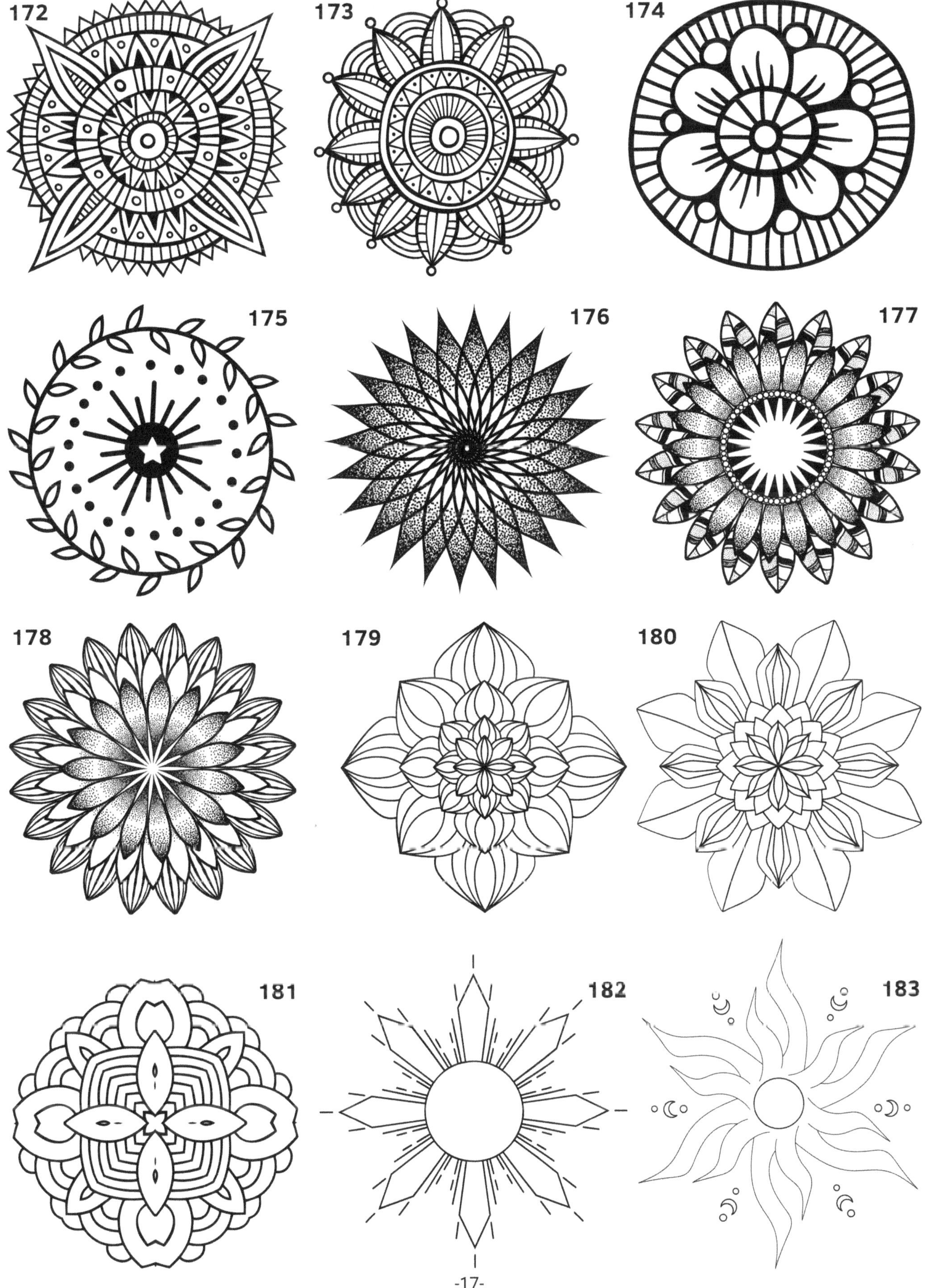

172
173
174
175
176
177
178
179
180
181
182
183

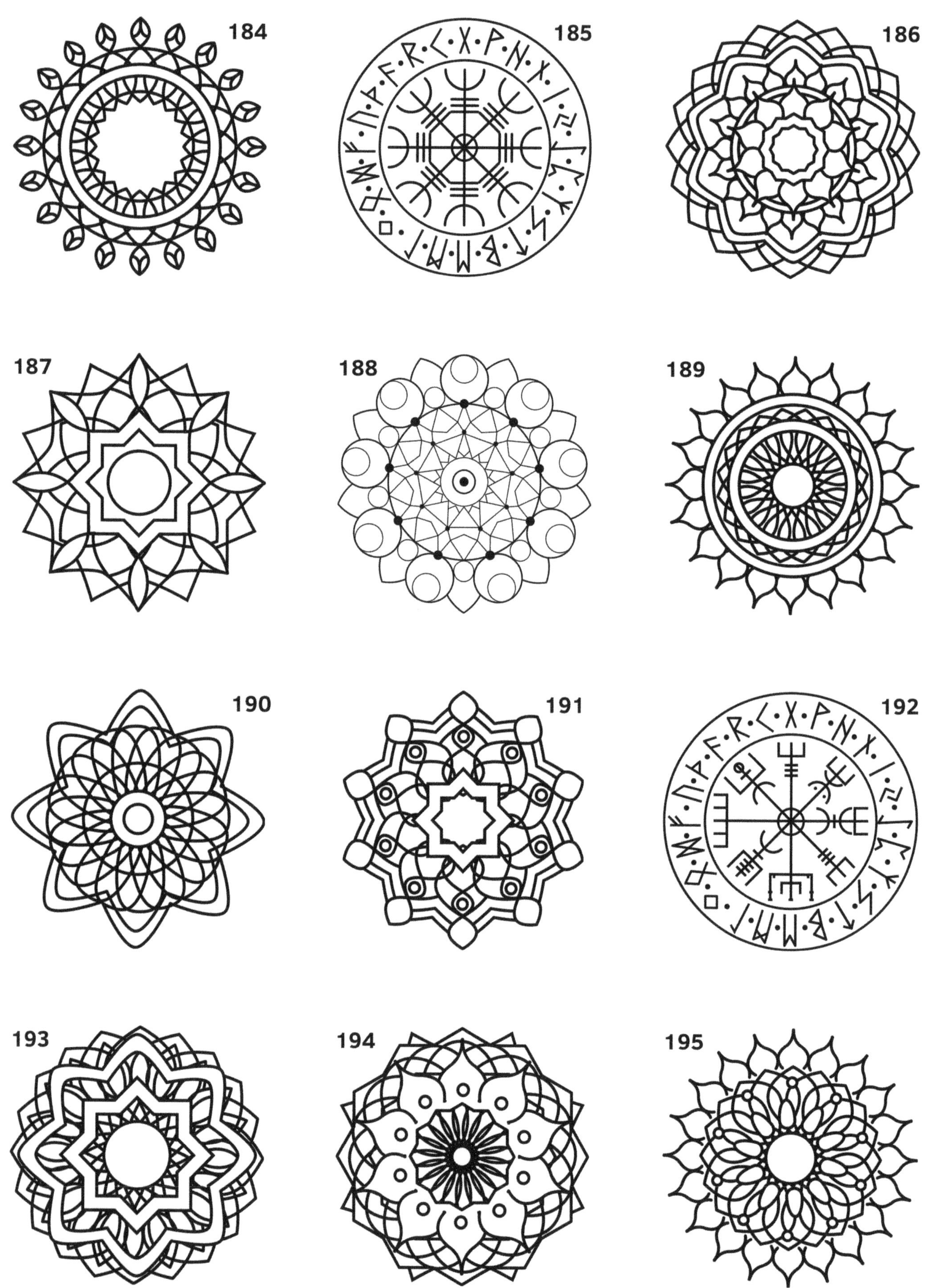

184
185
186
187
188
189
190
191
192
193
194
195

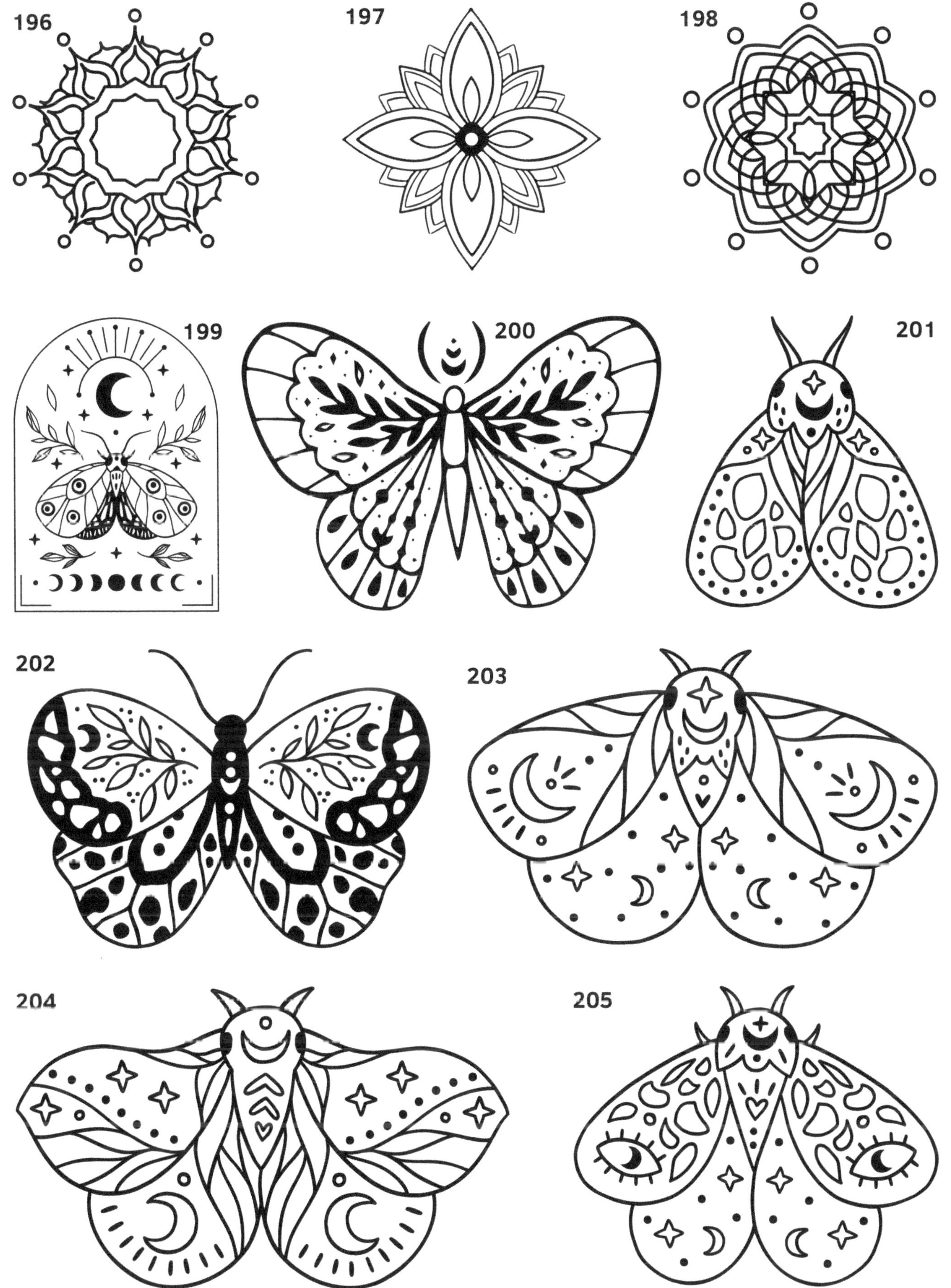

196
197
198
199
200
201
202
203
204
205

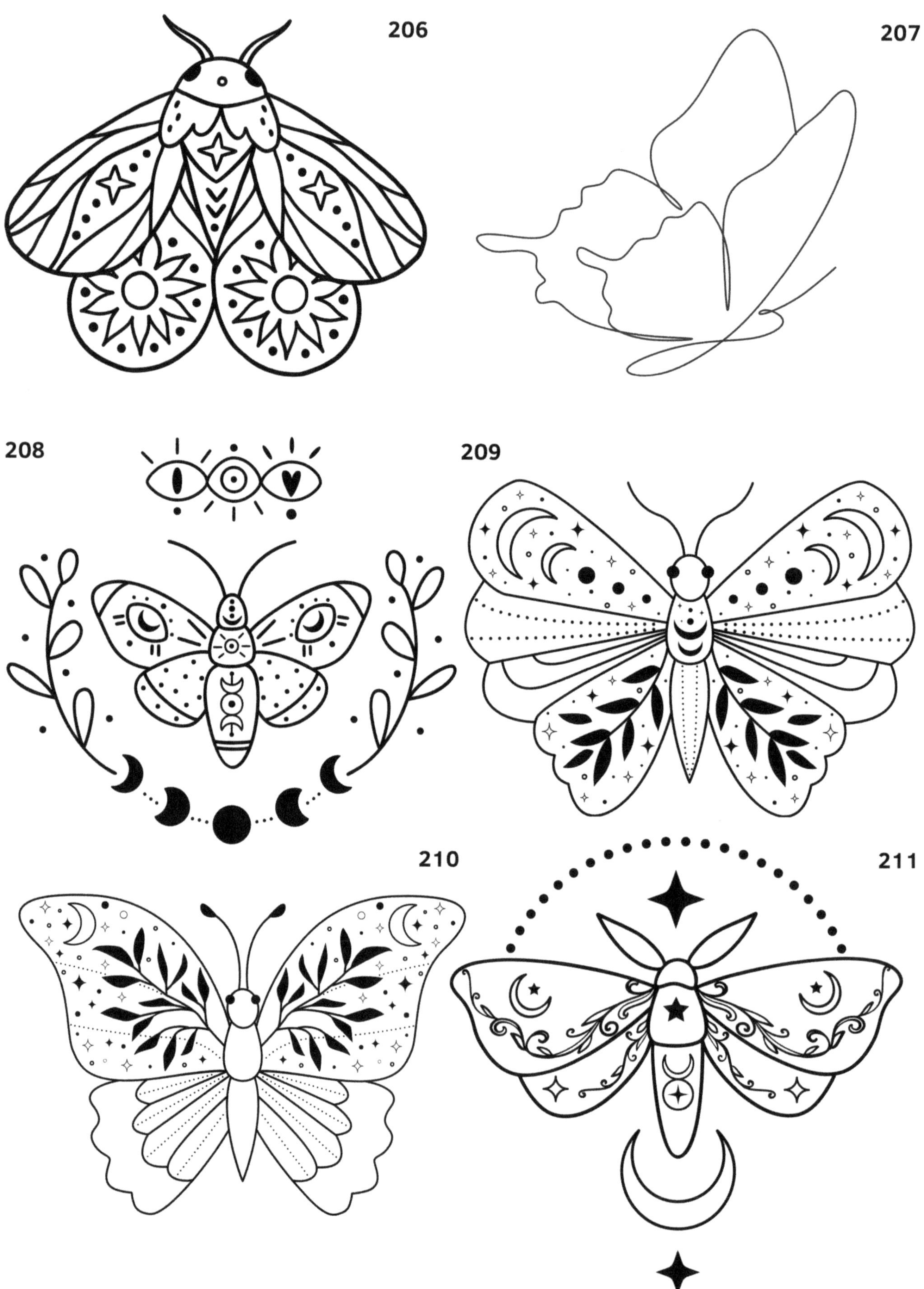

206
207
208
209
210
211

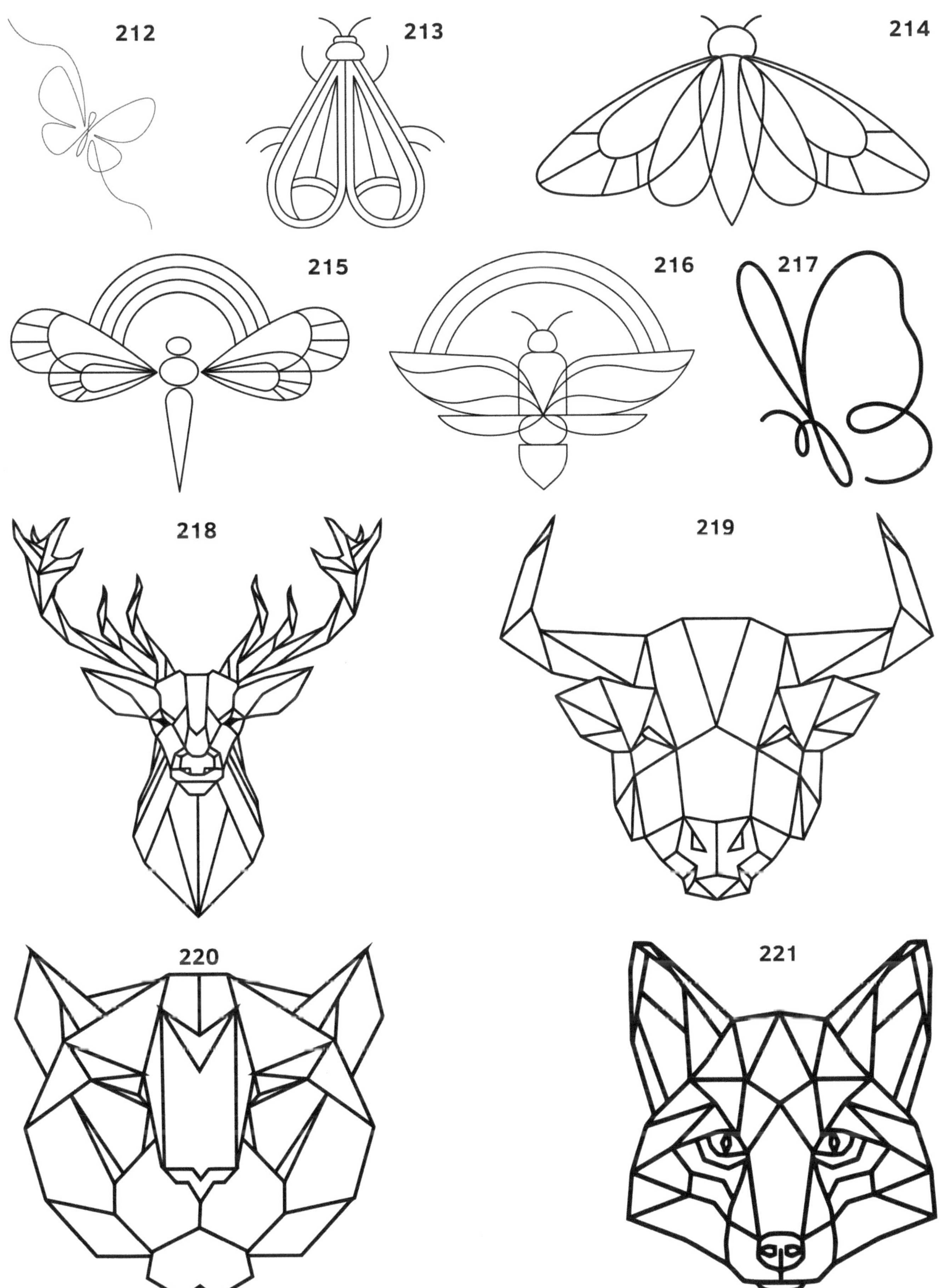
212
213
214
215
216
217
218
219
220
221

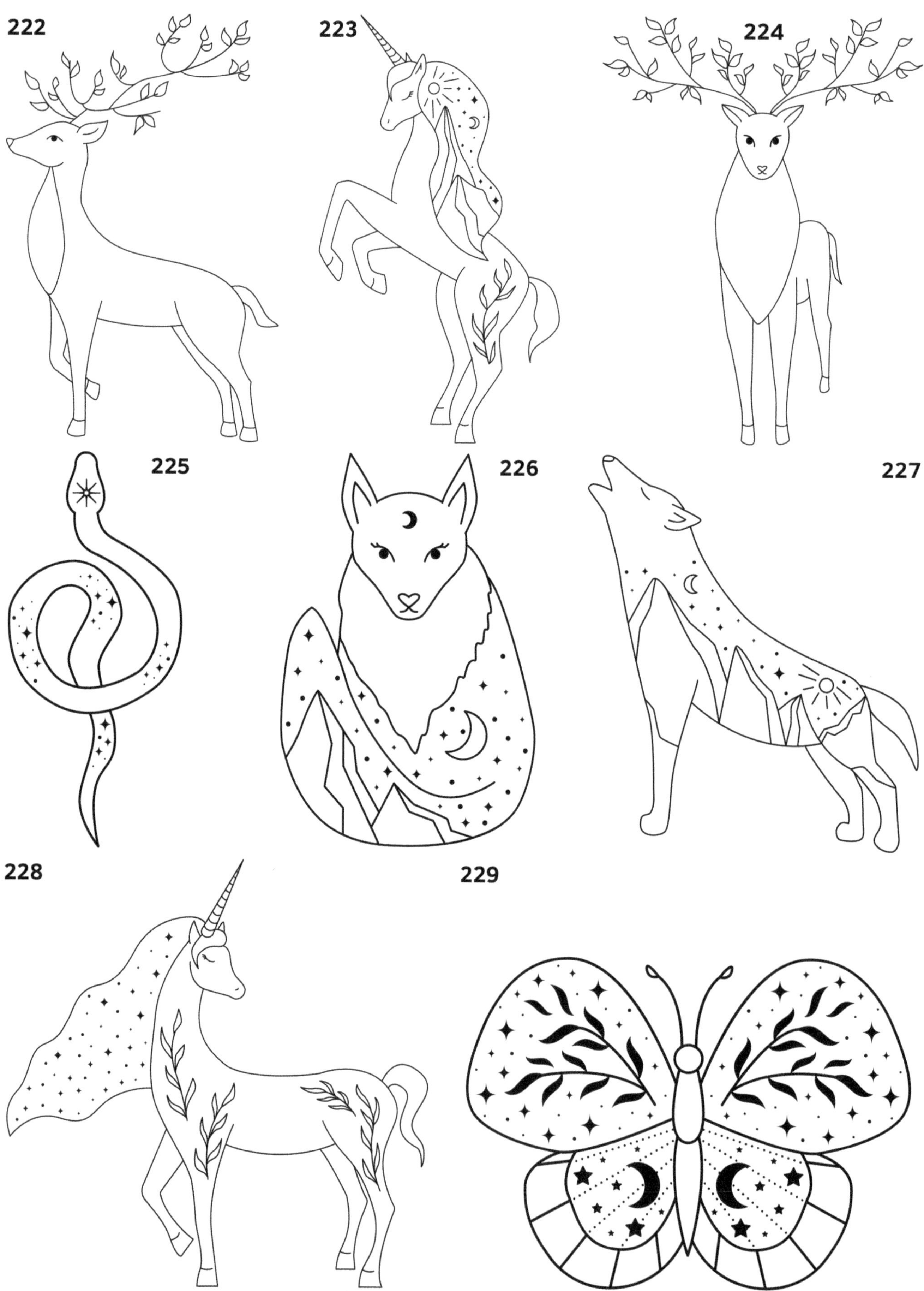

222
223
224
225
226
227
228
229

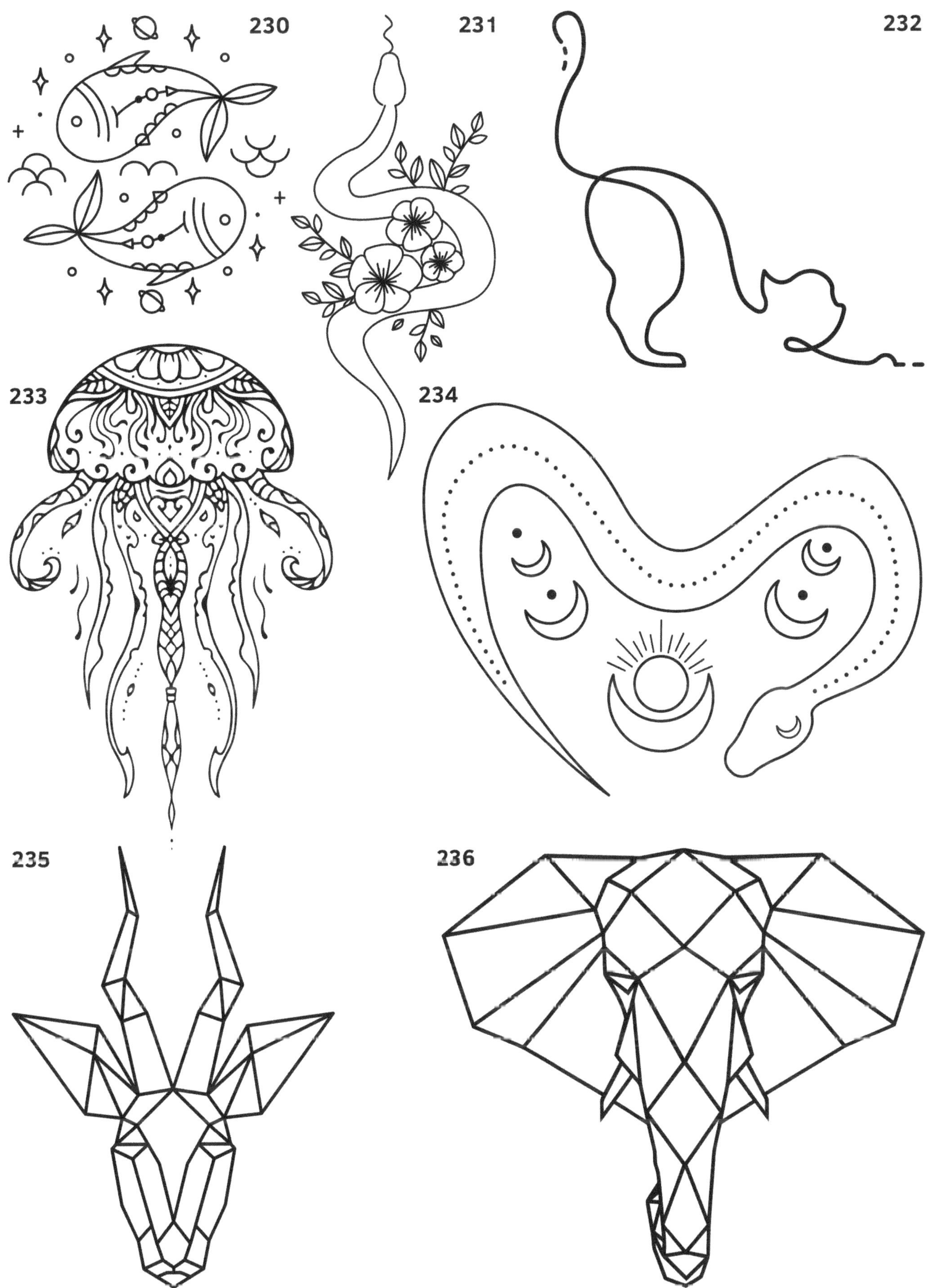

230

231

232

233

234

235

236

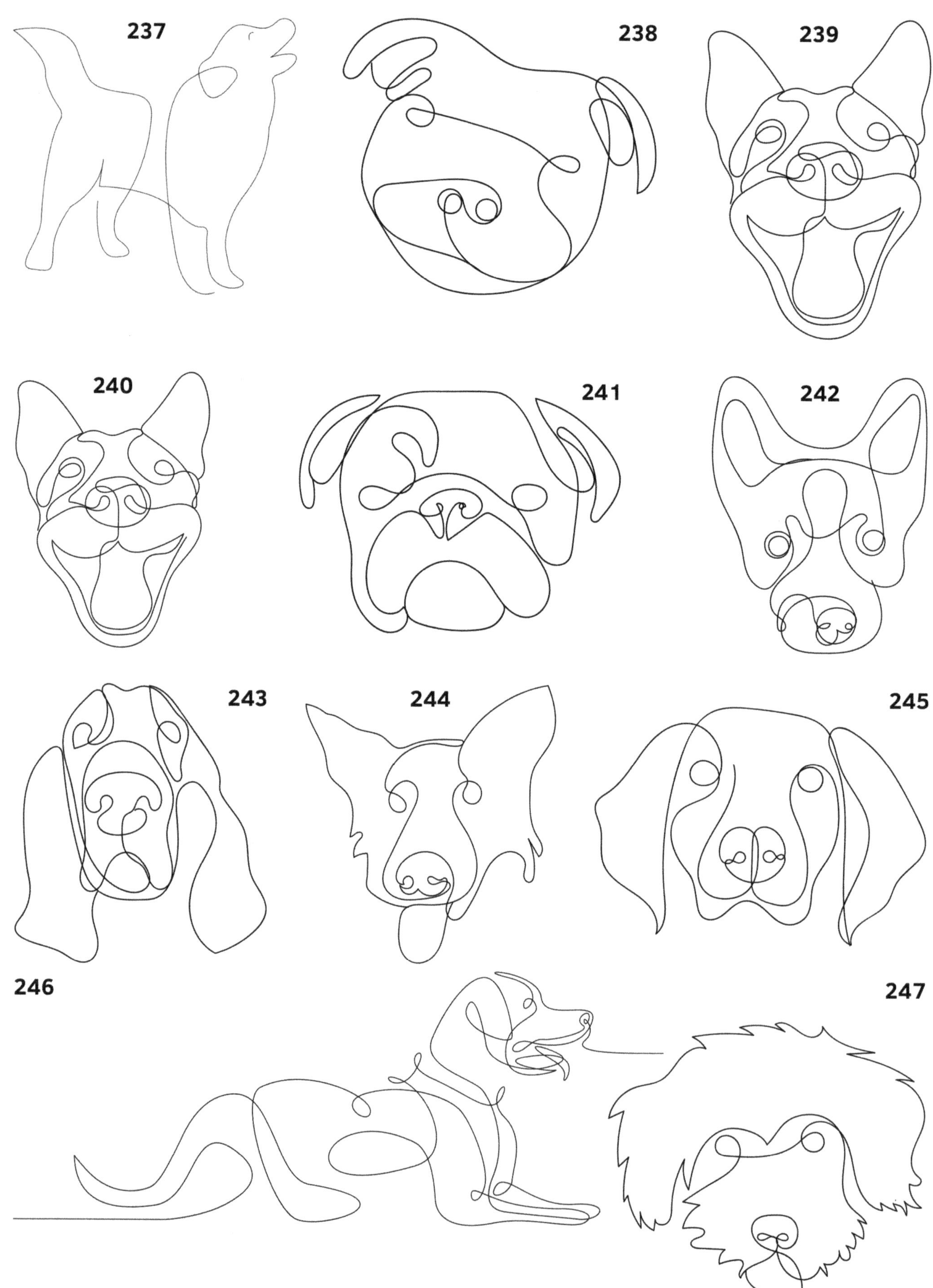
237
238
239
240
241
242
243
244
245
246
247

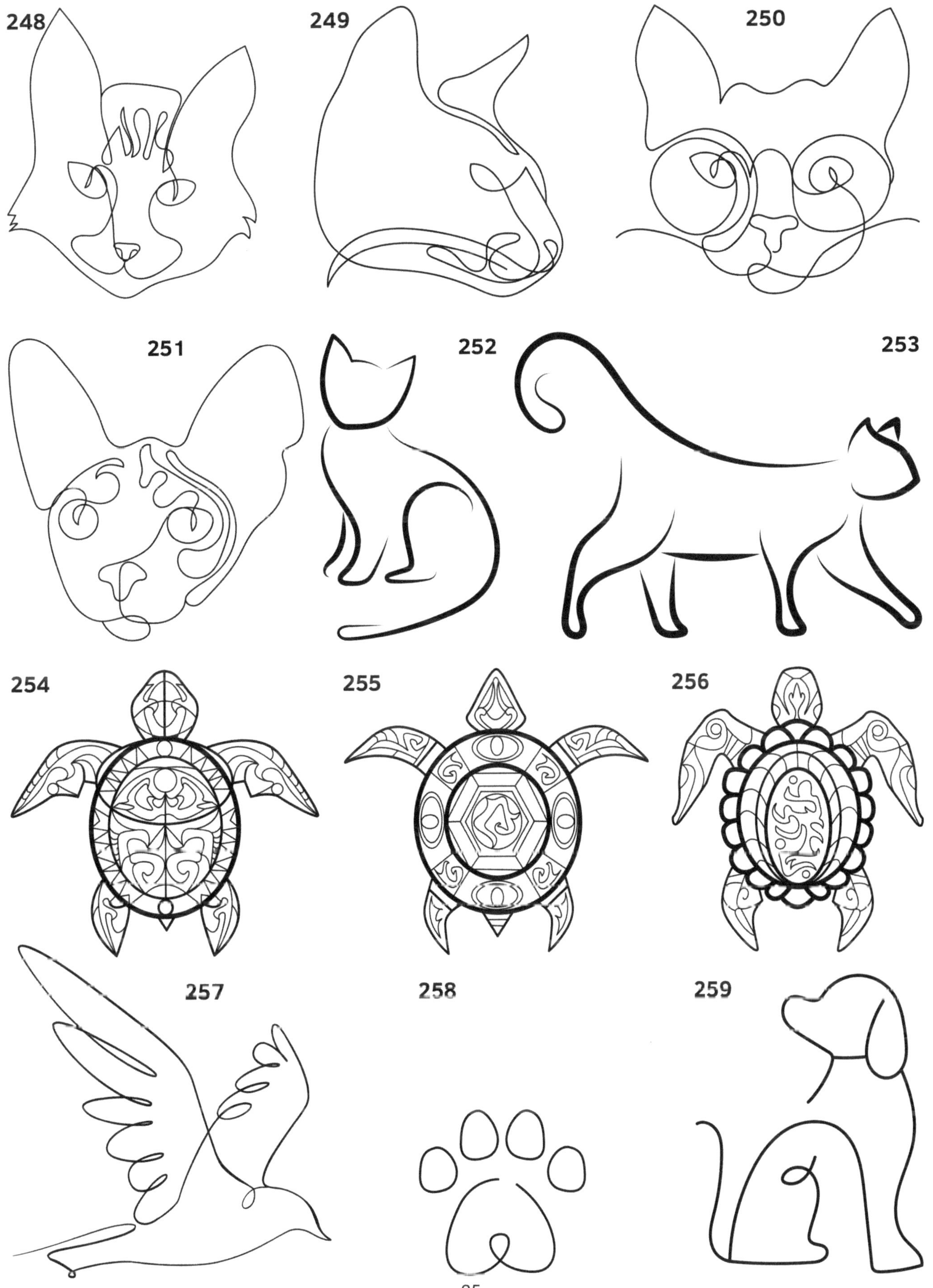

248
249
250
251
252
253
254
255
256
257
258
259

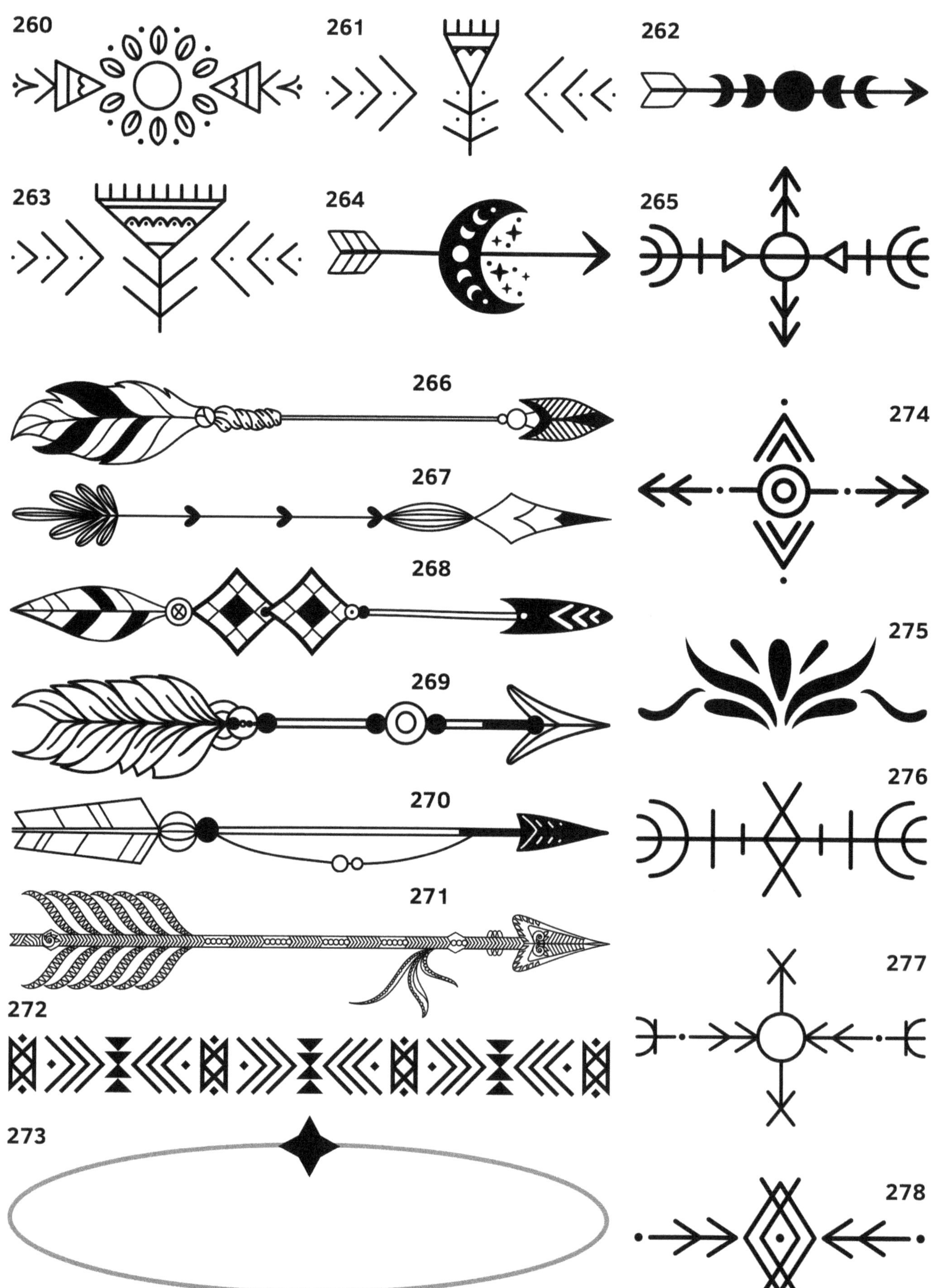

260
261
262
263
264
265
266
267
268
269
270
271
272
273
274
275
276
277
278

279

280

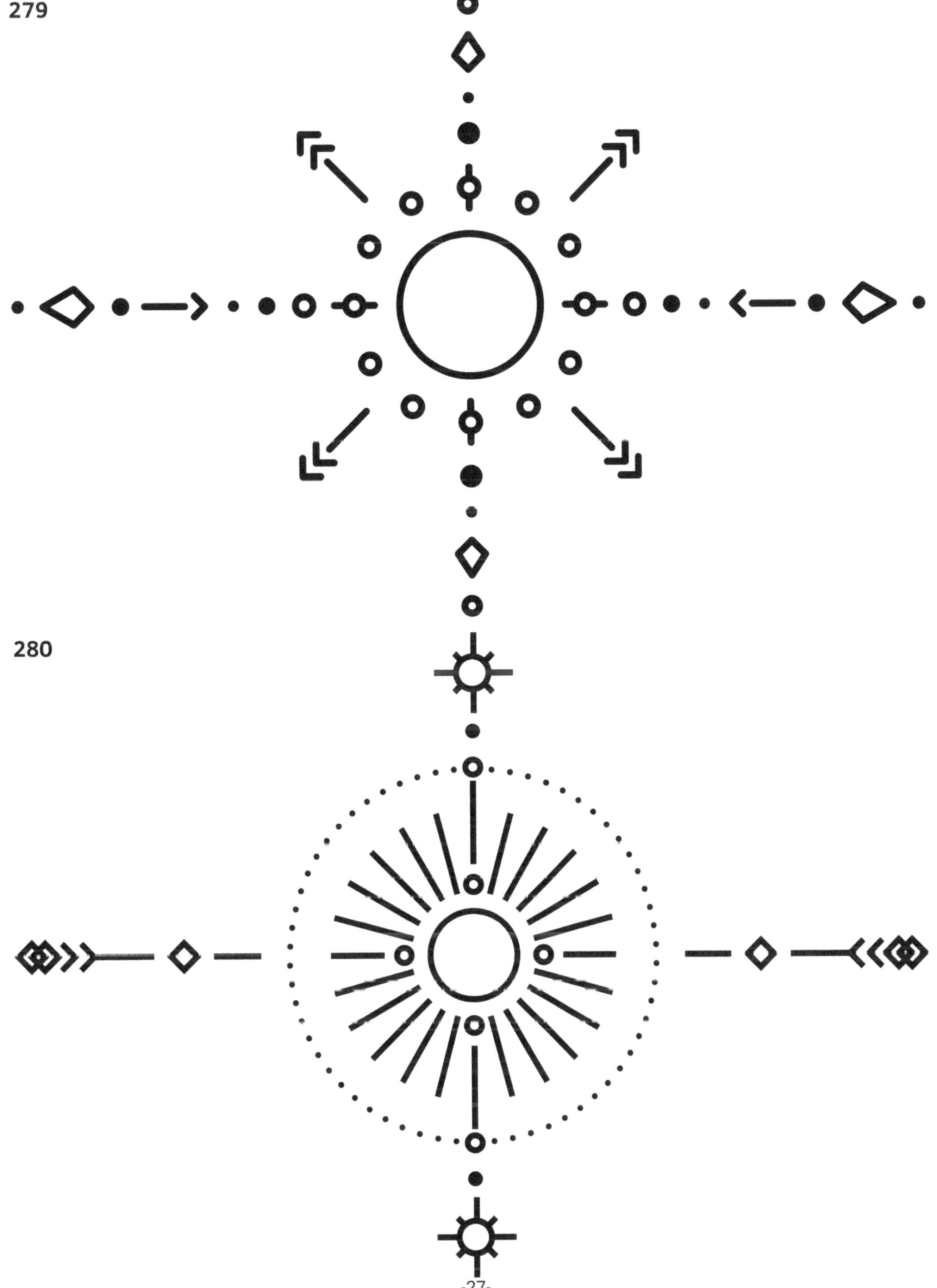

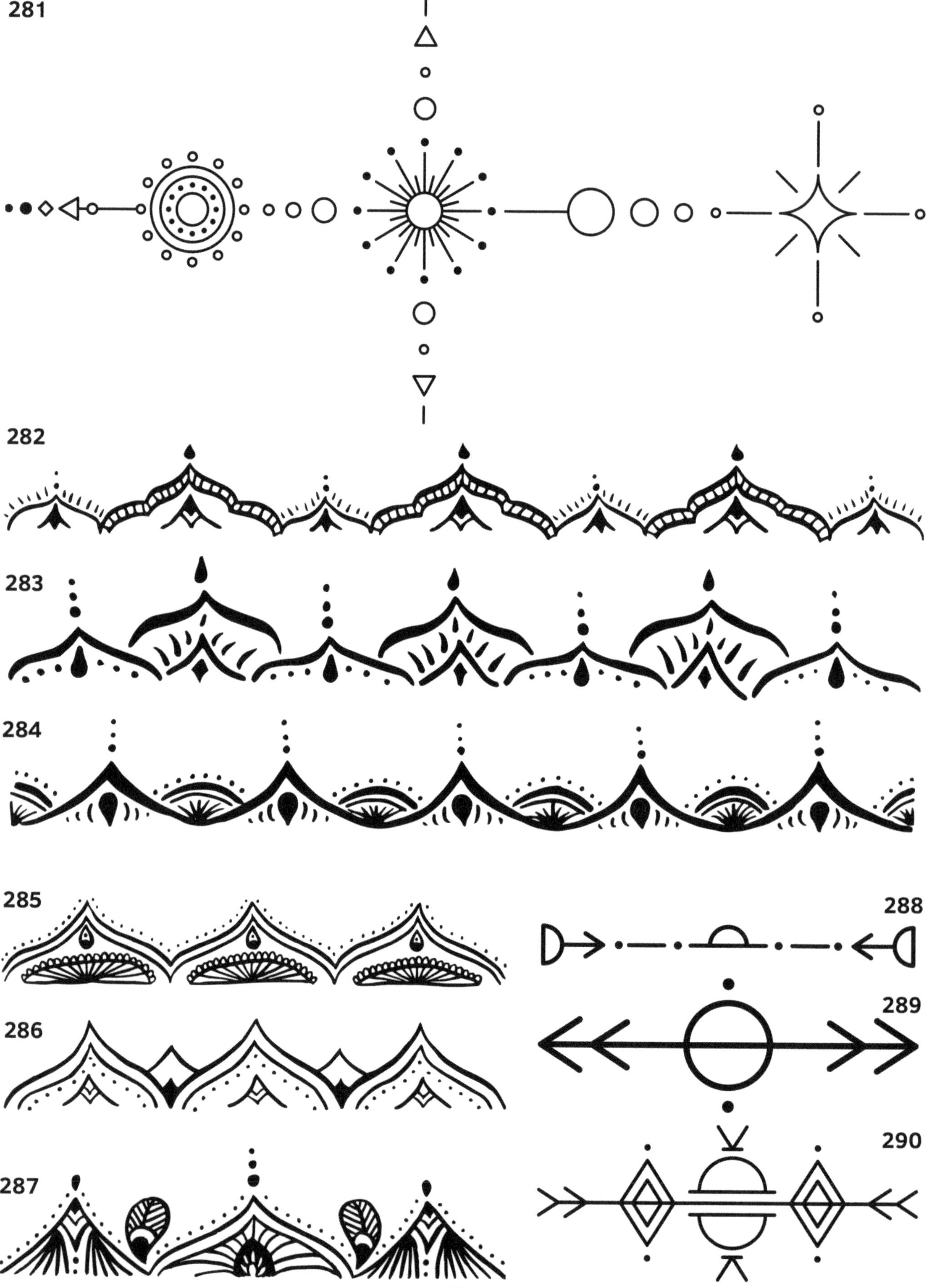

281
282
283
284
285
286
287
288
289
290

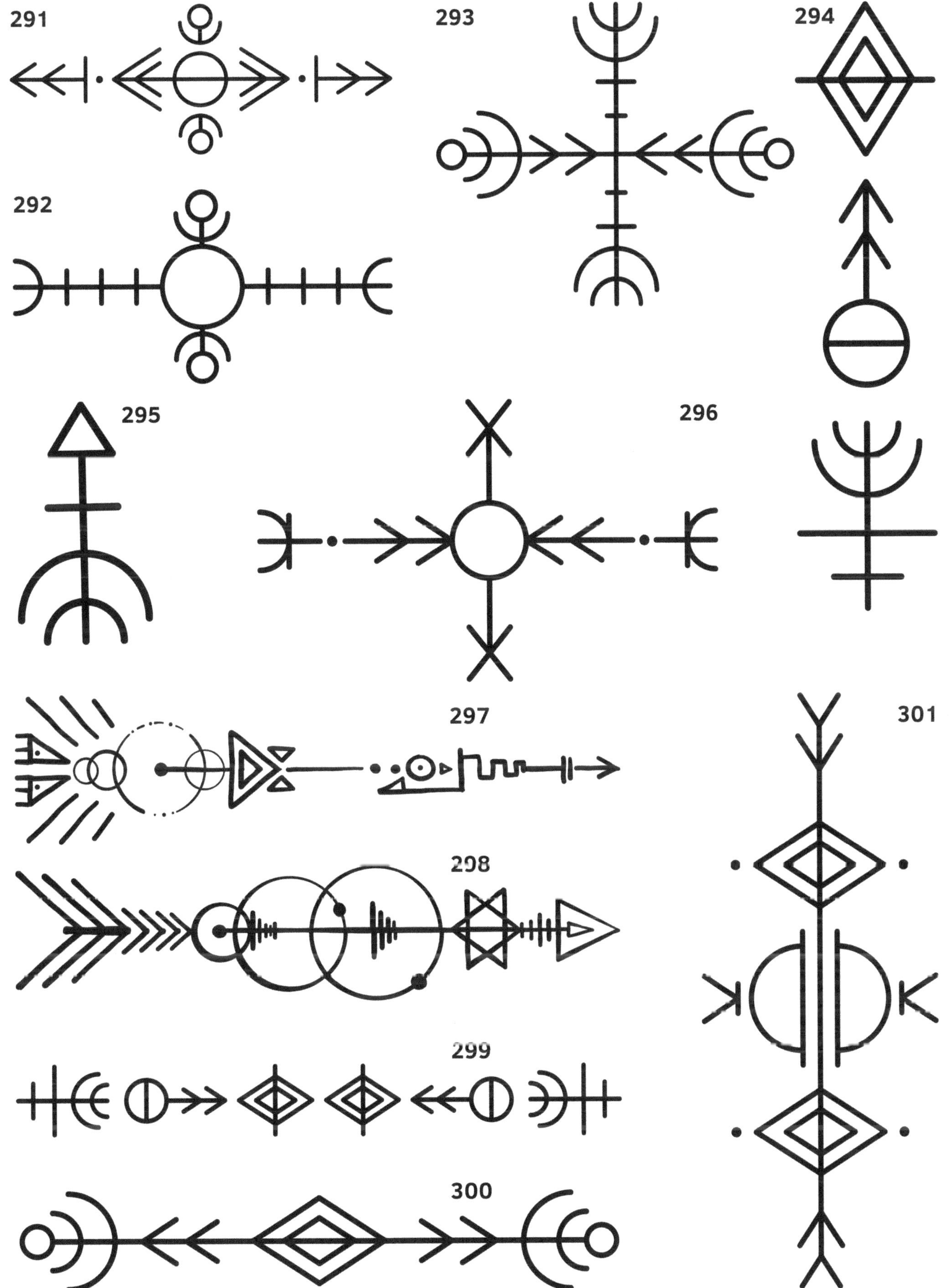

291
292
293
294
295
296
297
298
299
300
301

302

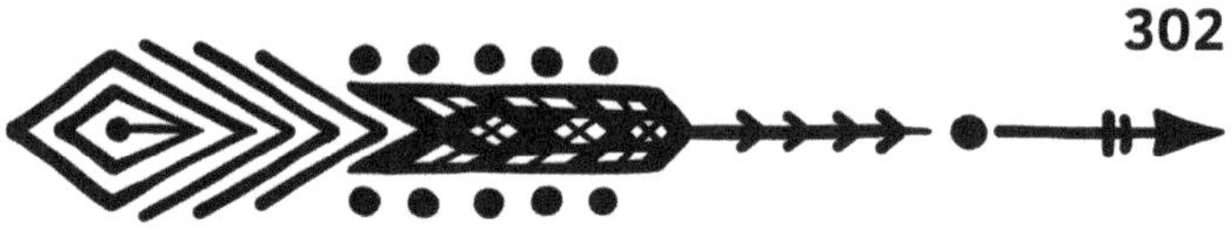

303

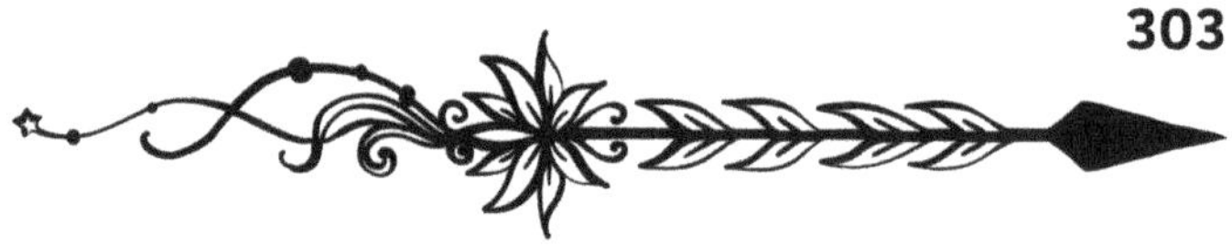

304

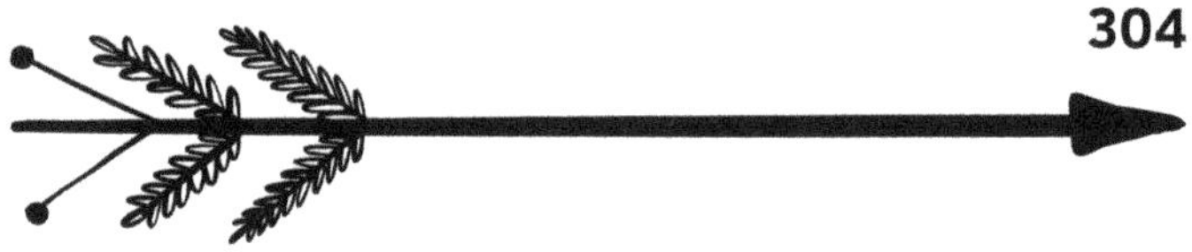

305

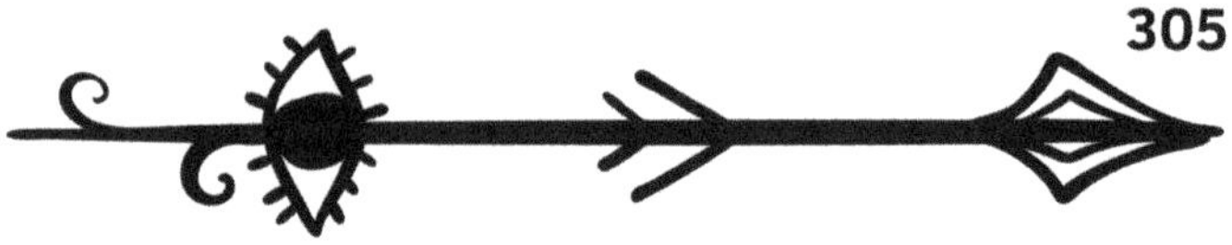

306

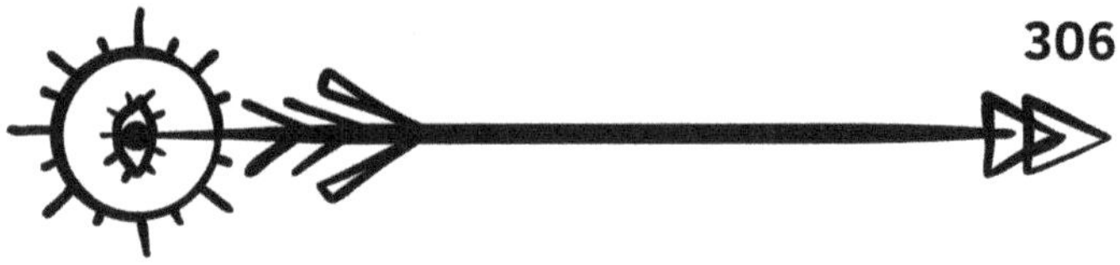

307

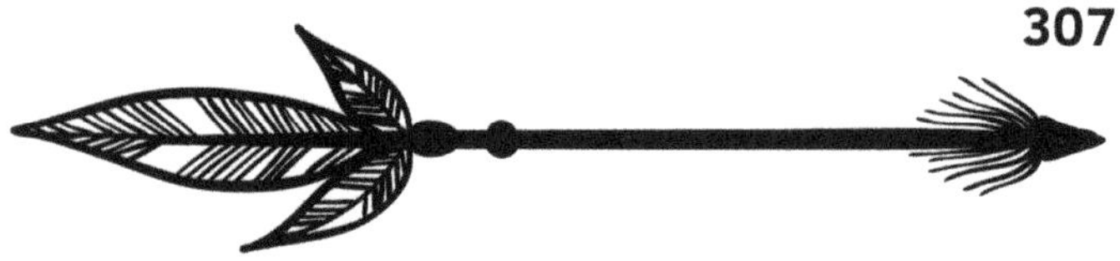

308

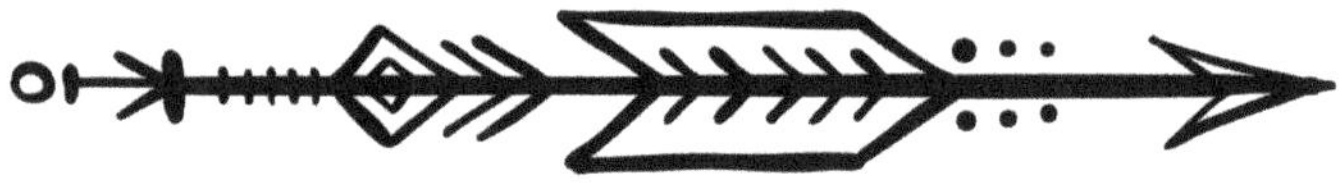

309

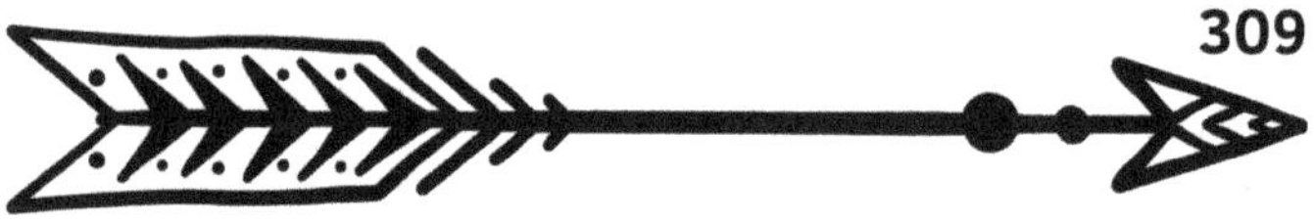

310

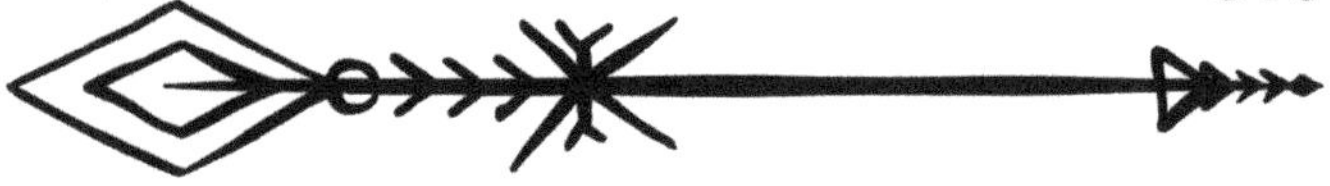

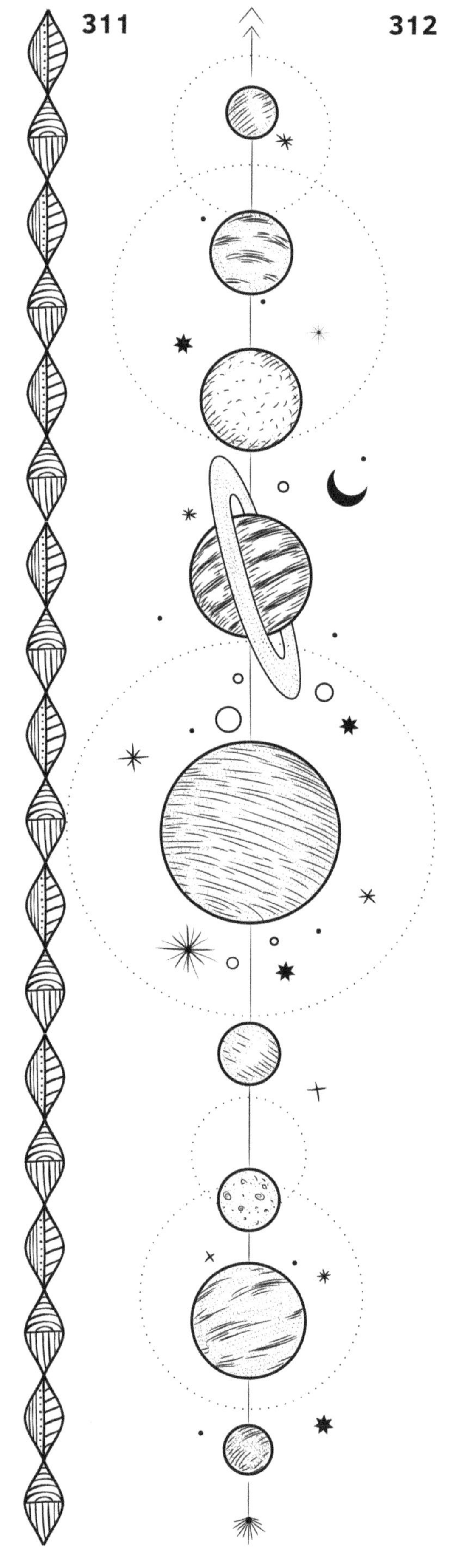

311

312

313

314

315

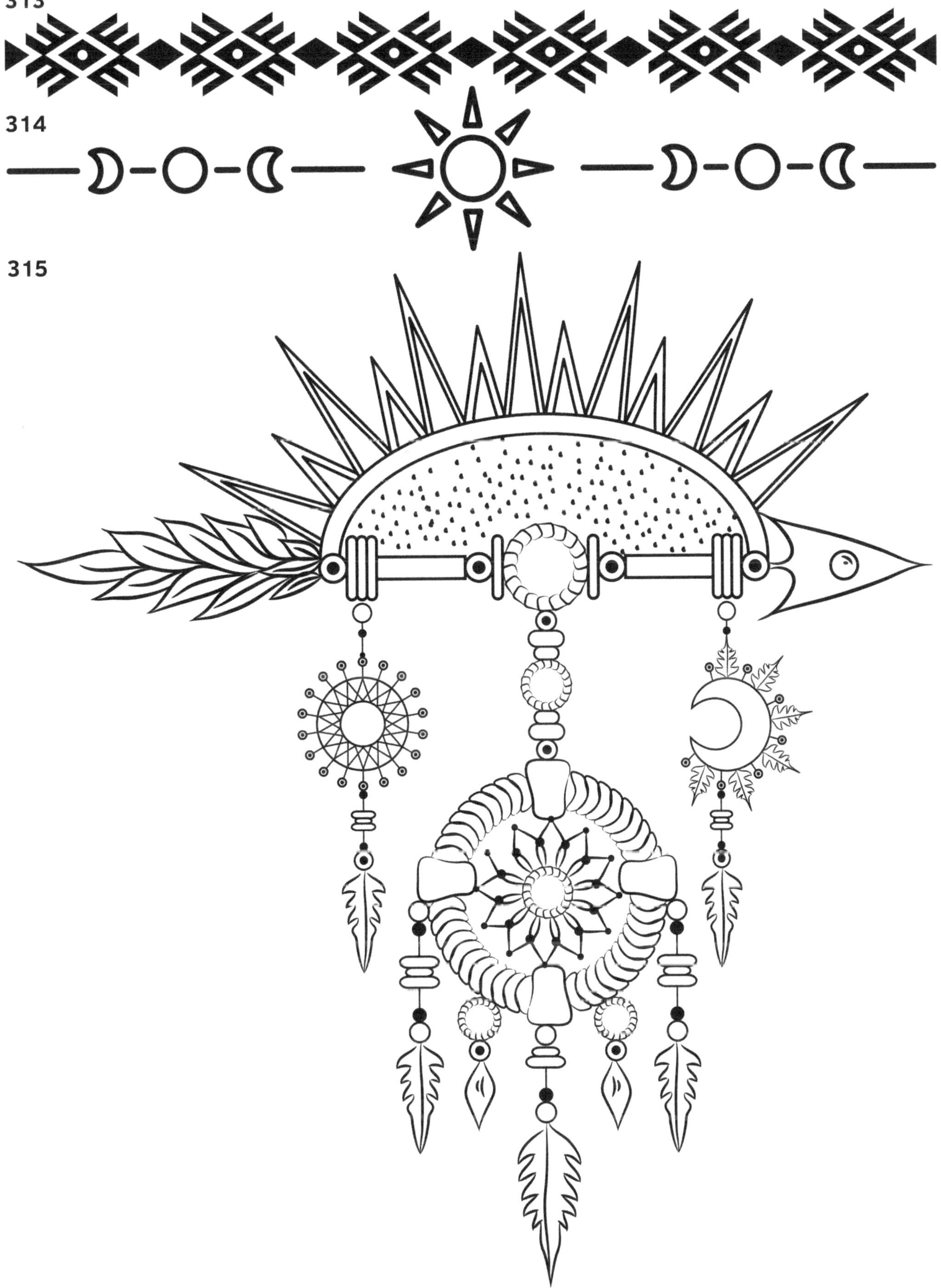

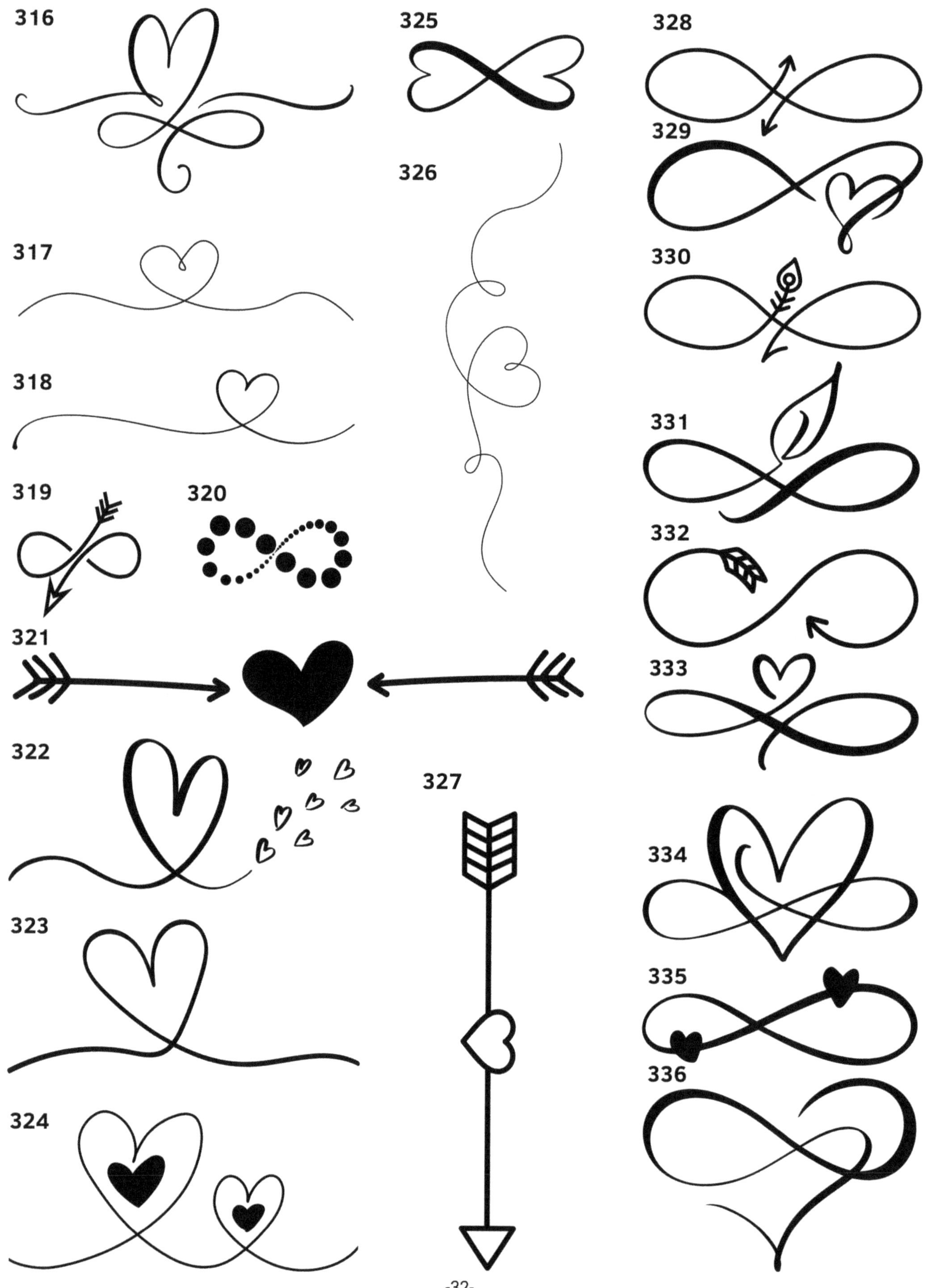

316
317
318
319
320
321
322
323
324
325
326
327
328
329
330
331
332
333
334
335
336

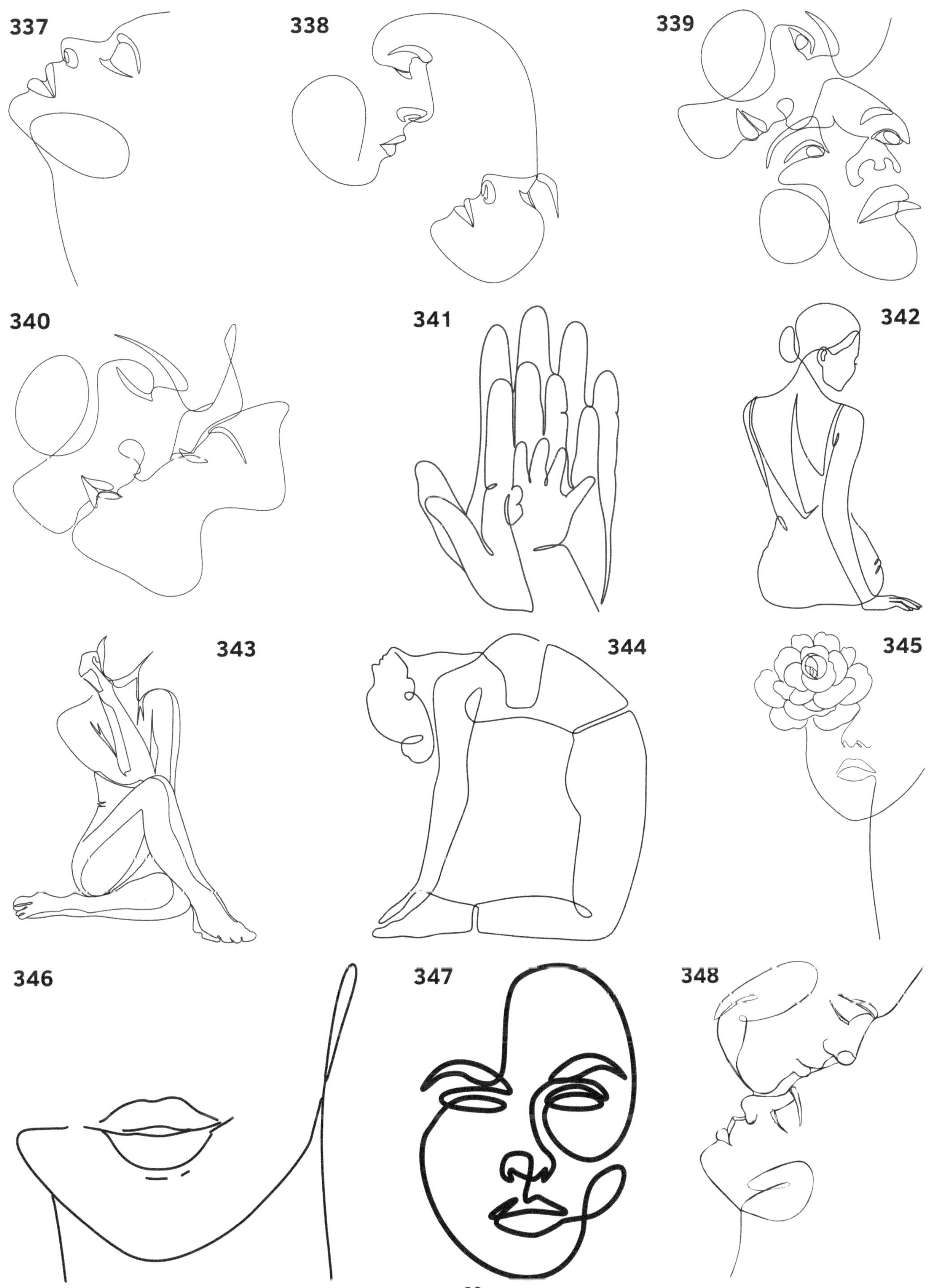

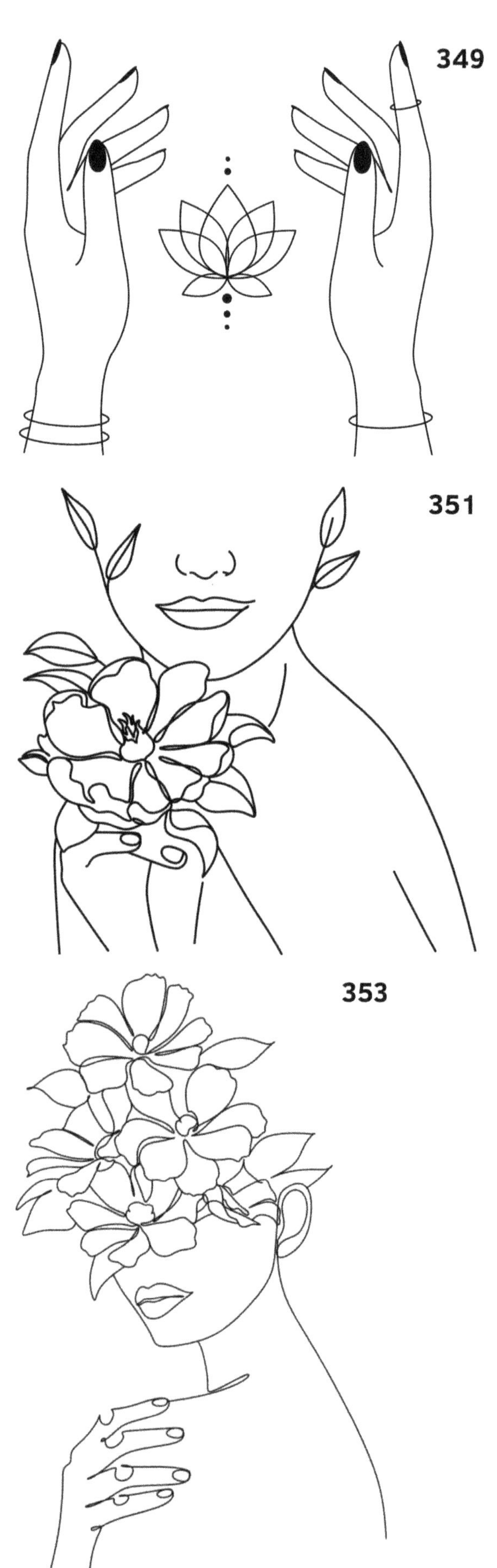
349
351
353

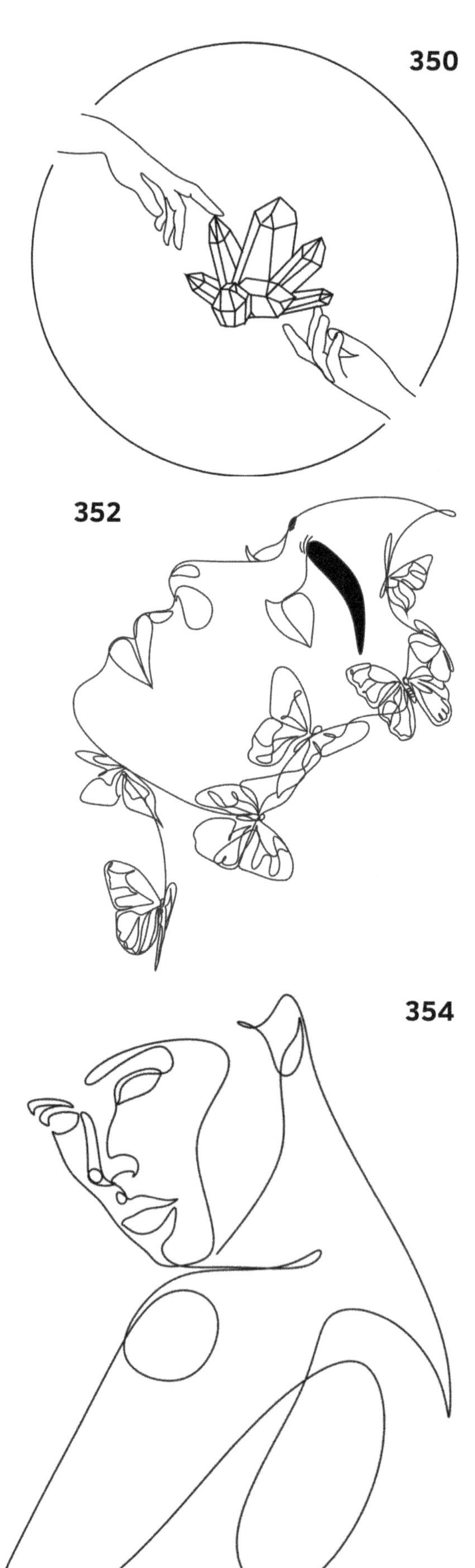
350
352
354

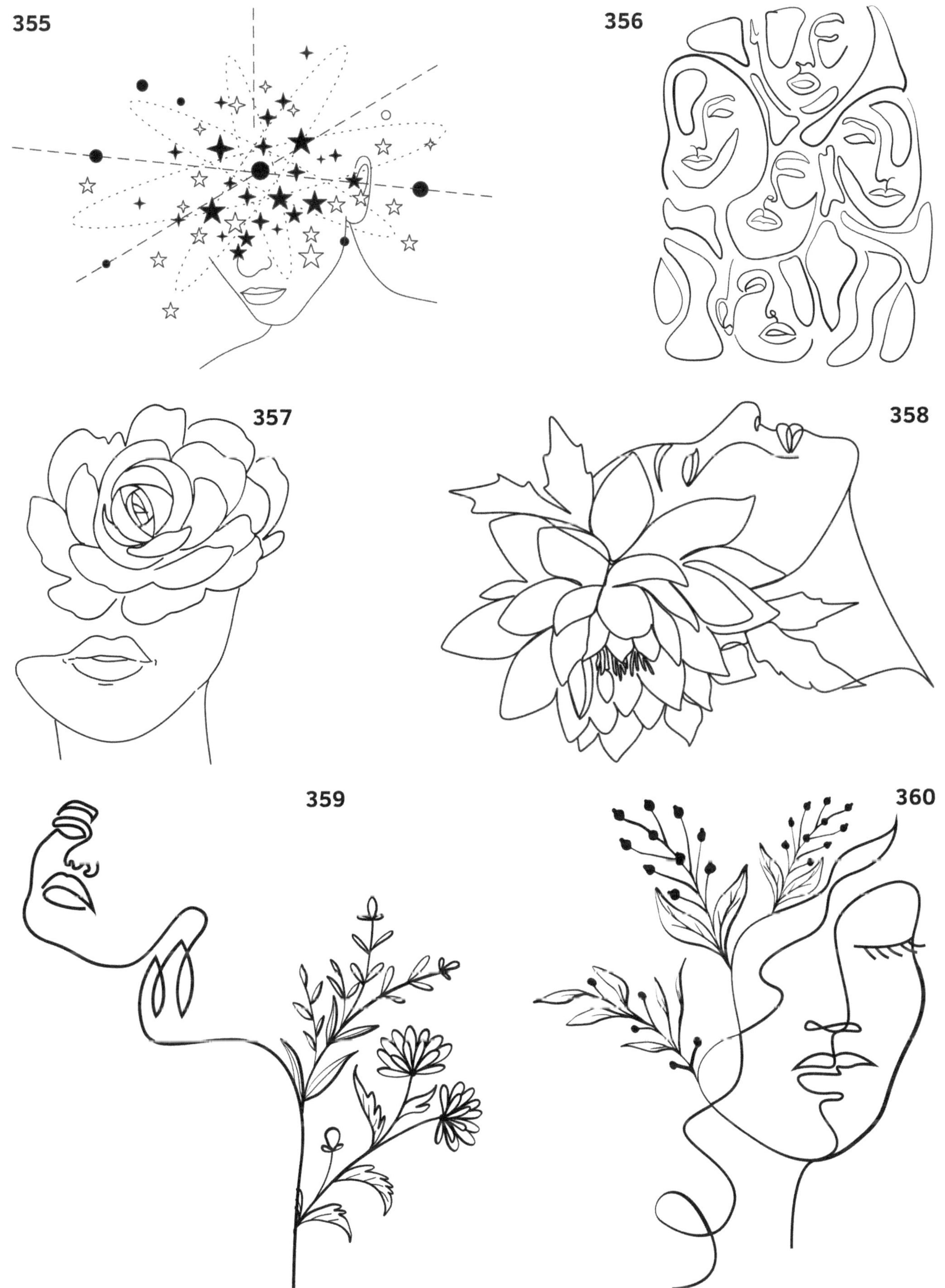

355
356
357
358
359
360

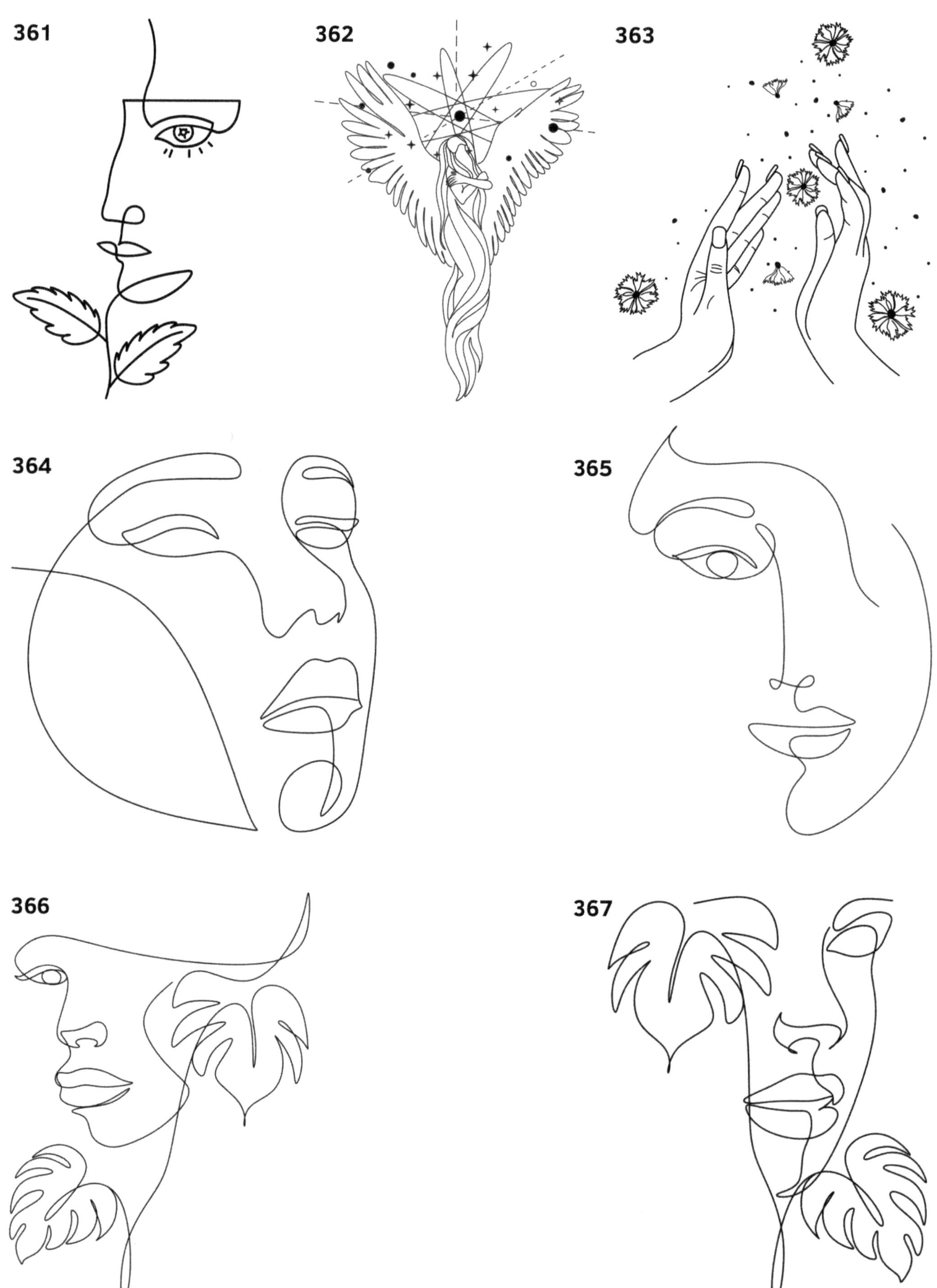

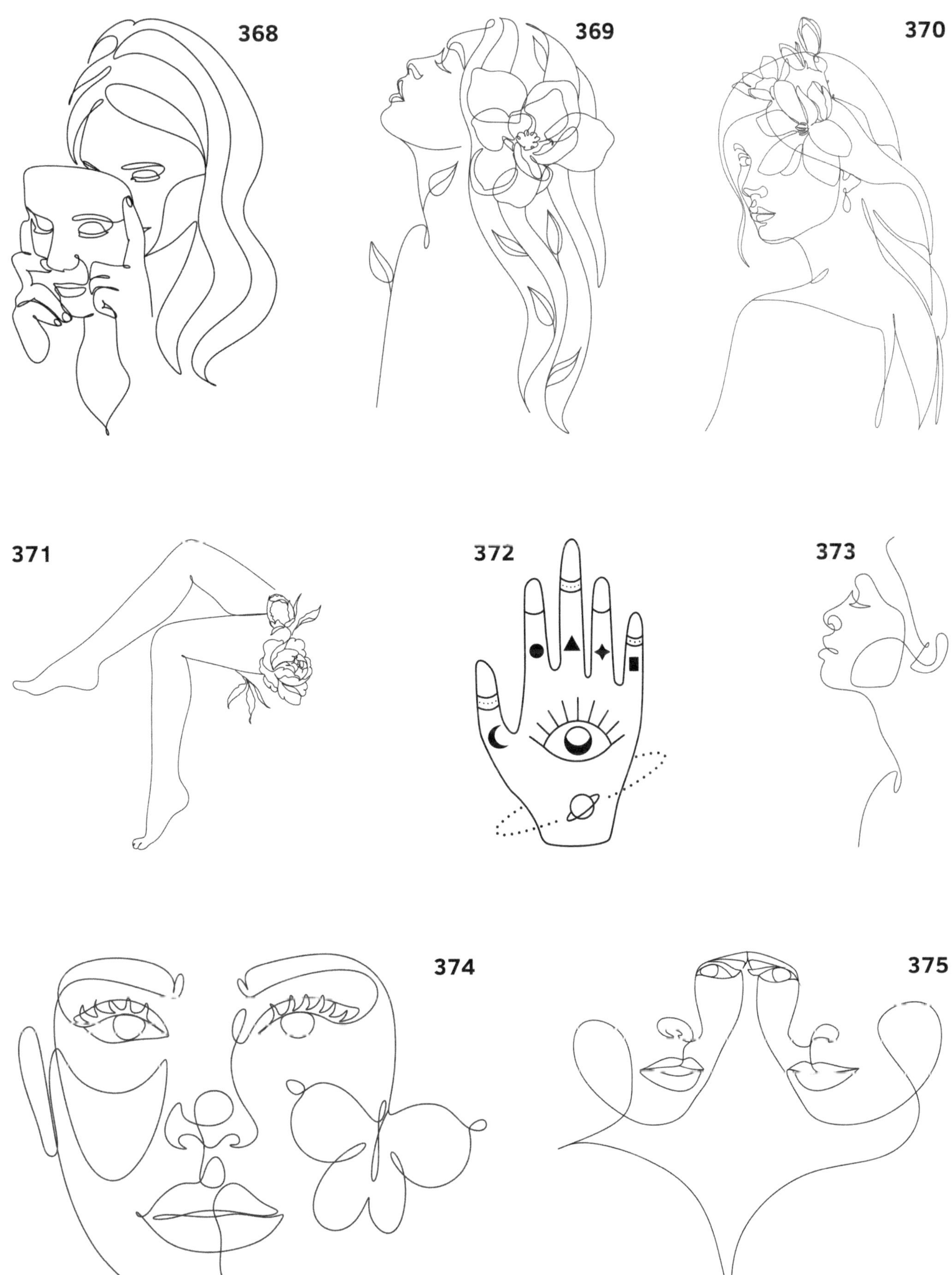

368
369
370
371
372
373
374
375

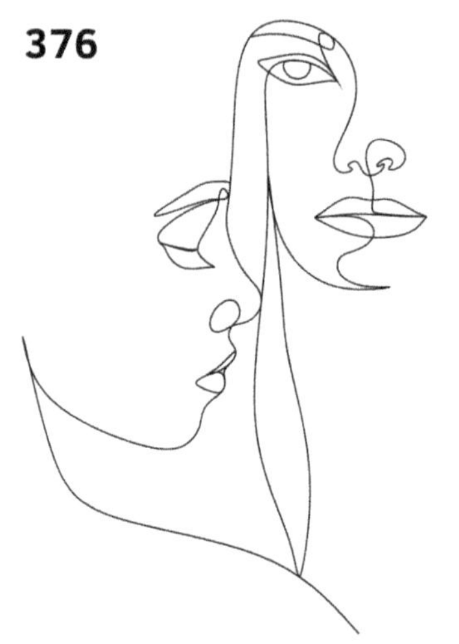

376

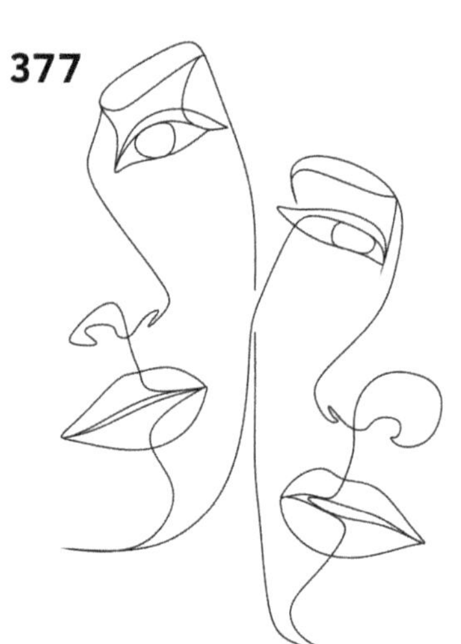

377

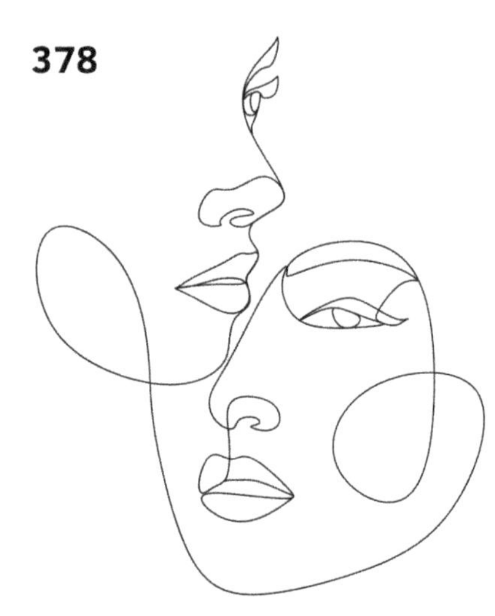

378

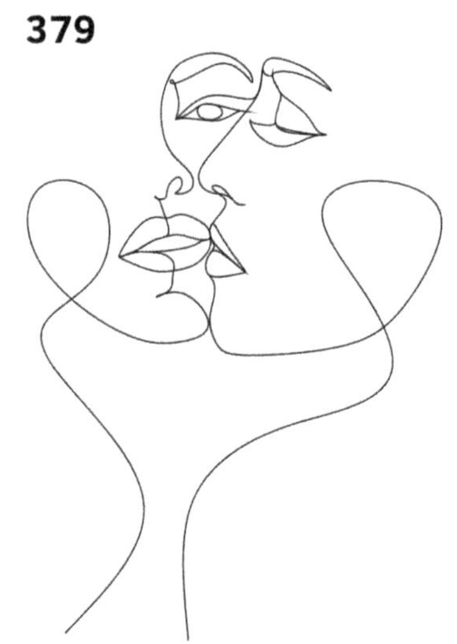

379

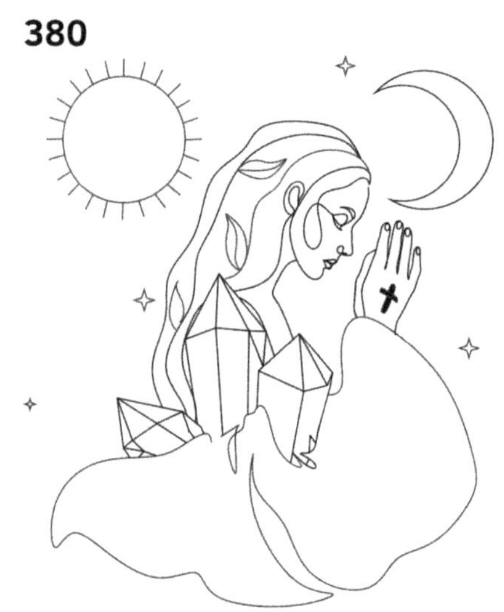

380

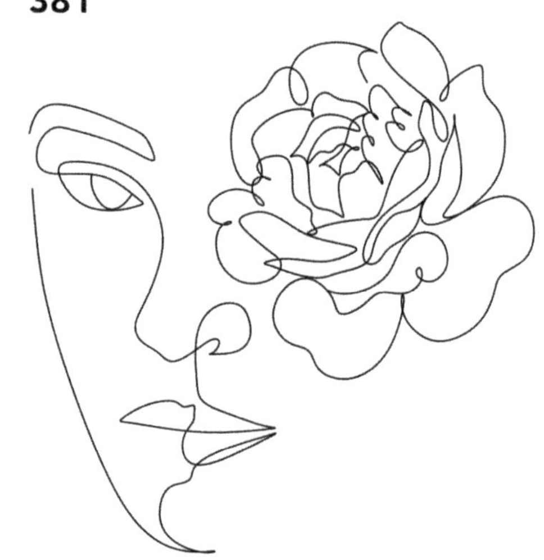

381

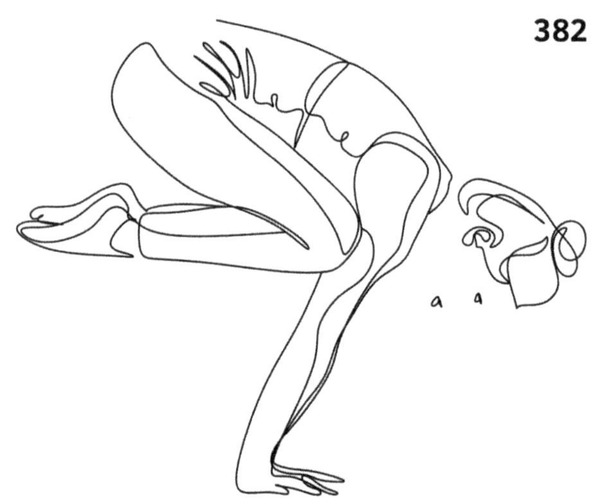

382

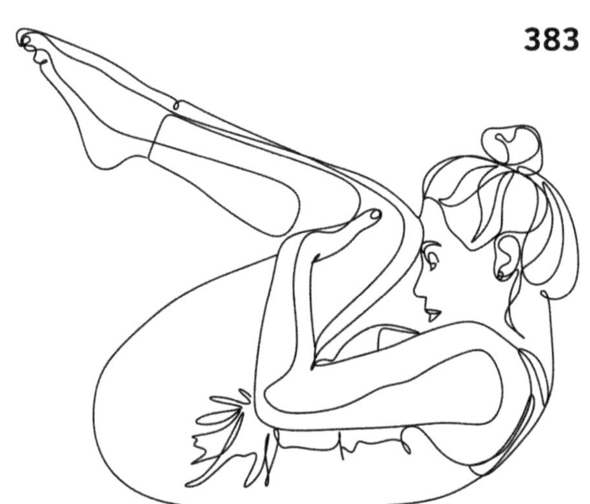

383

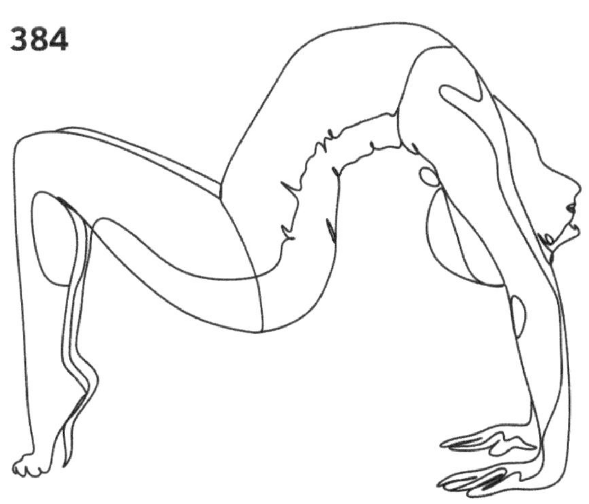

384

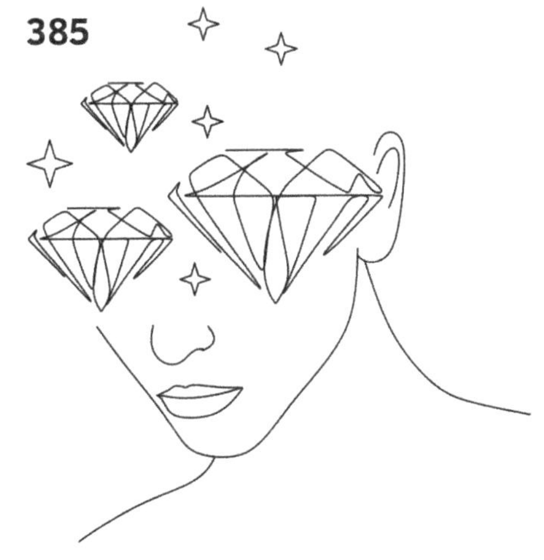

385

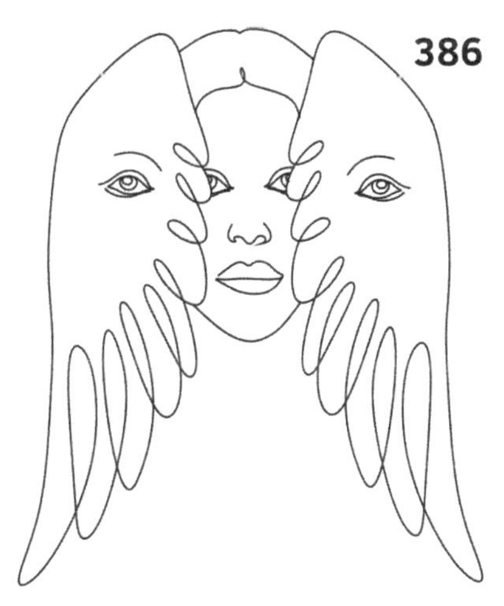

386

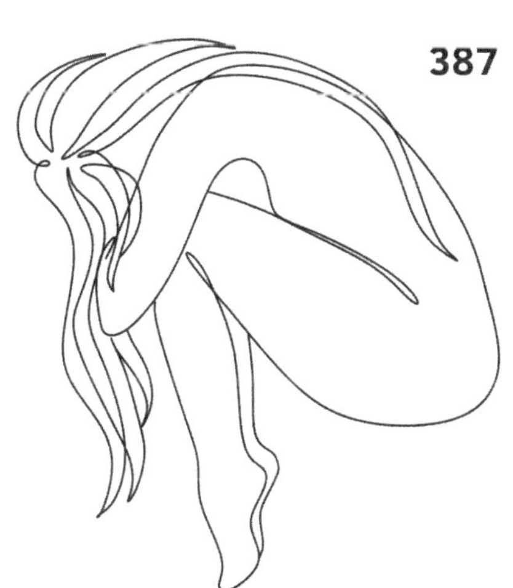

387

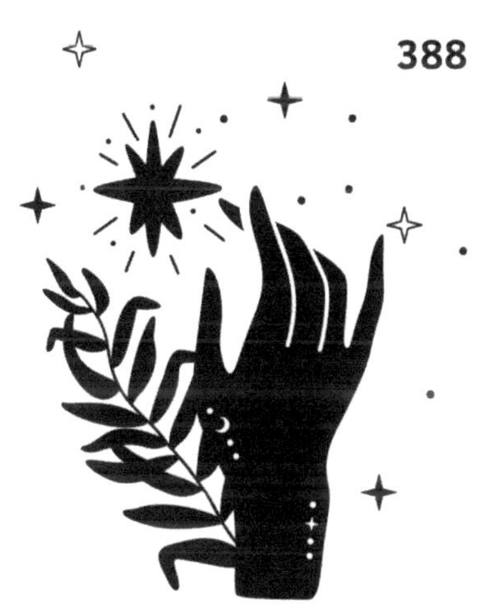

388

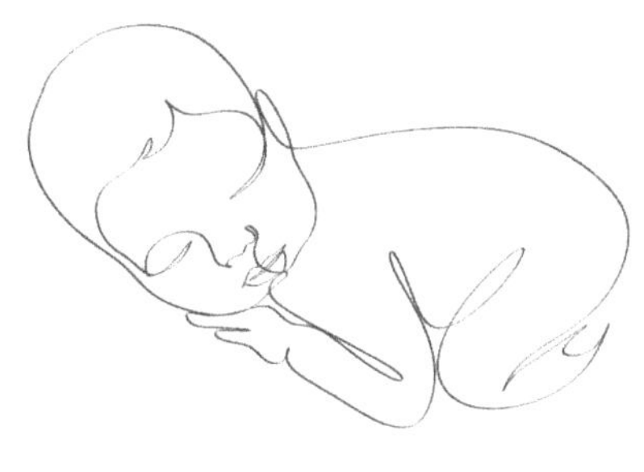

389

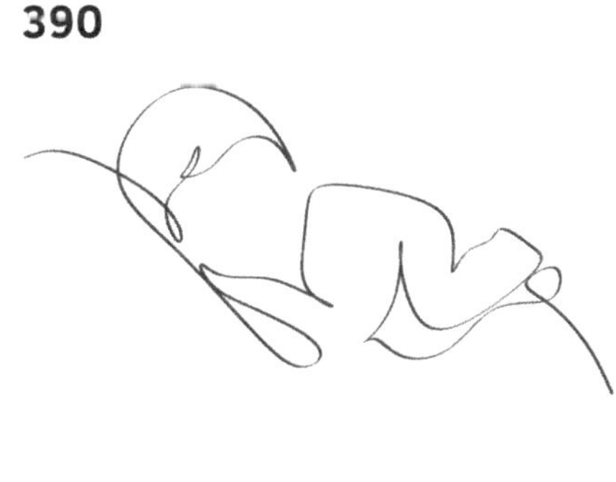

390

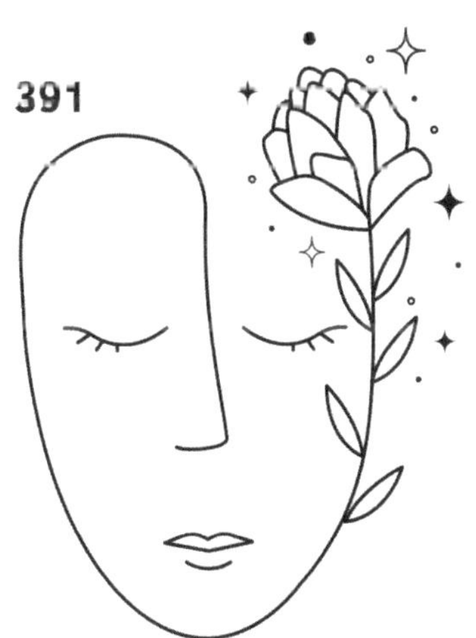

391

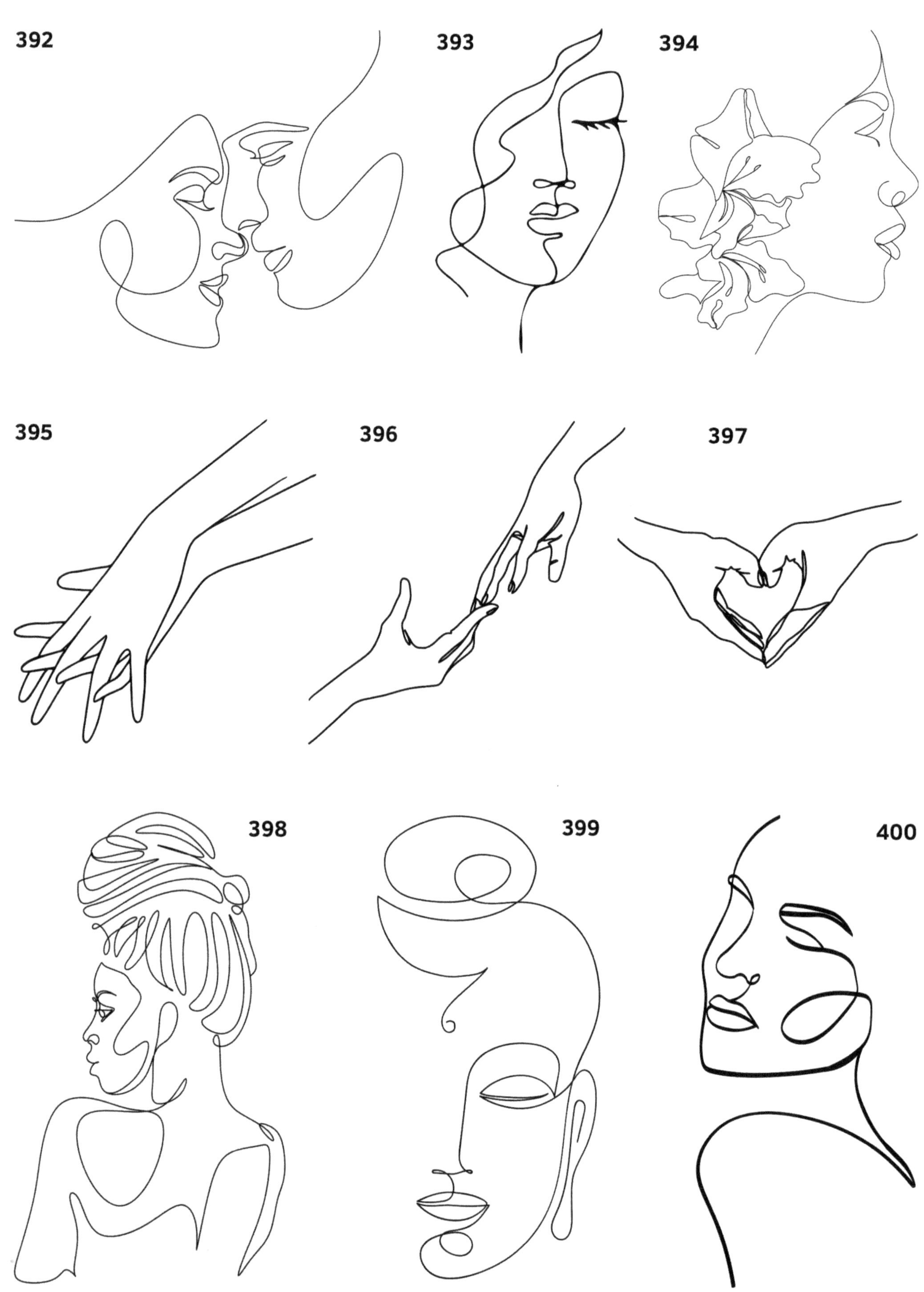

392
393
394
395
396
397
398
399
400

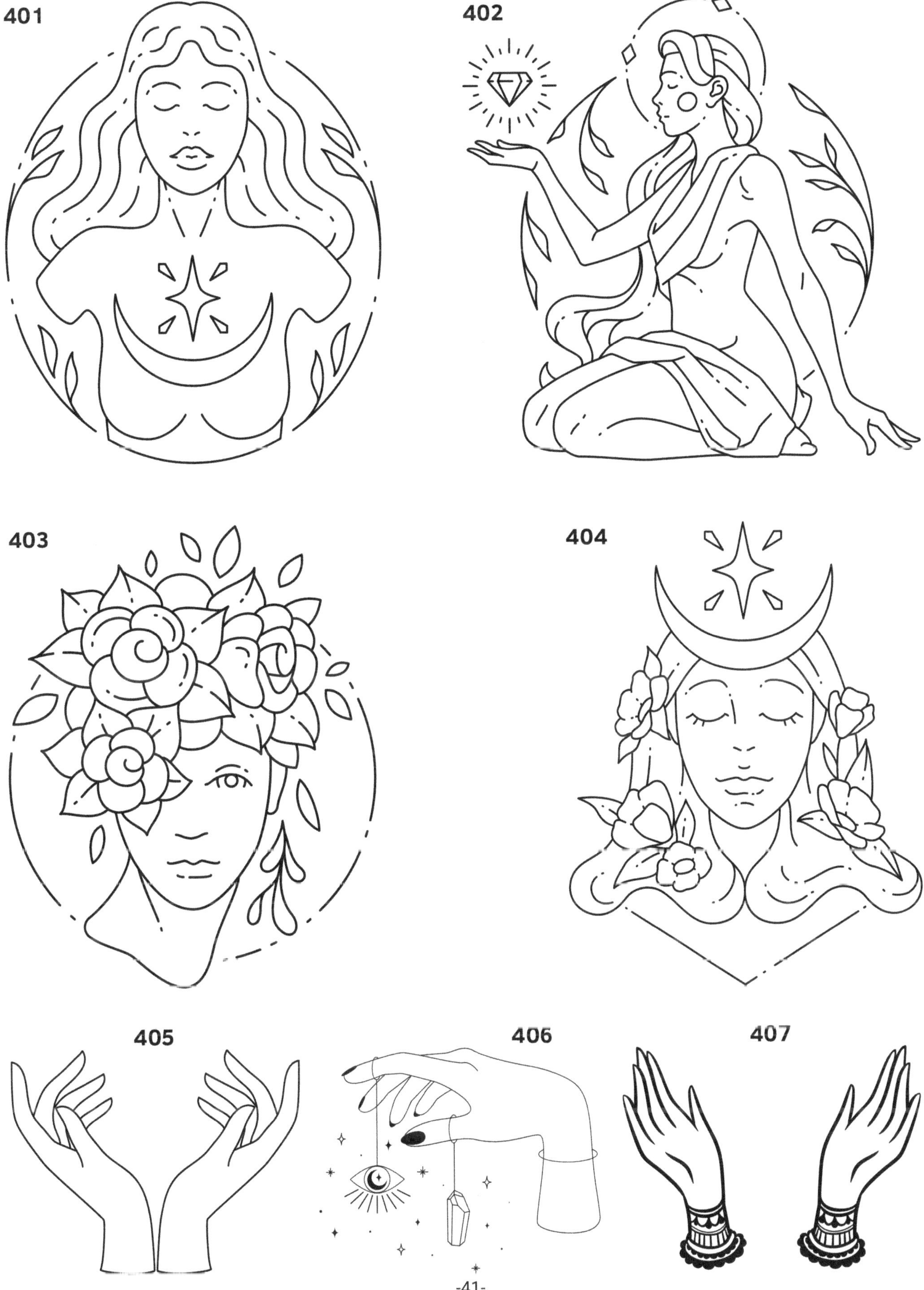
401
402
403
404
405
406
407

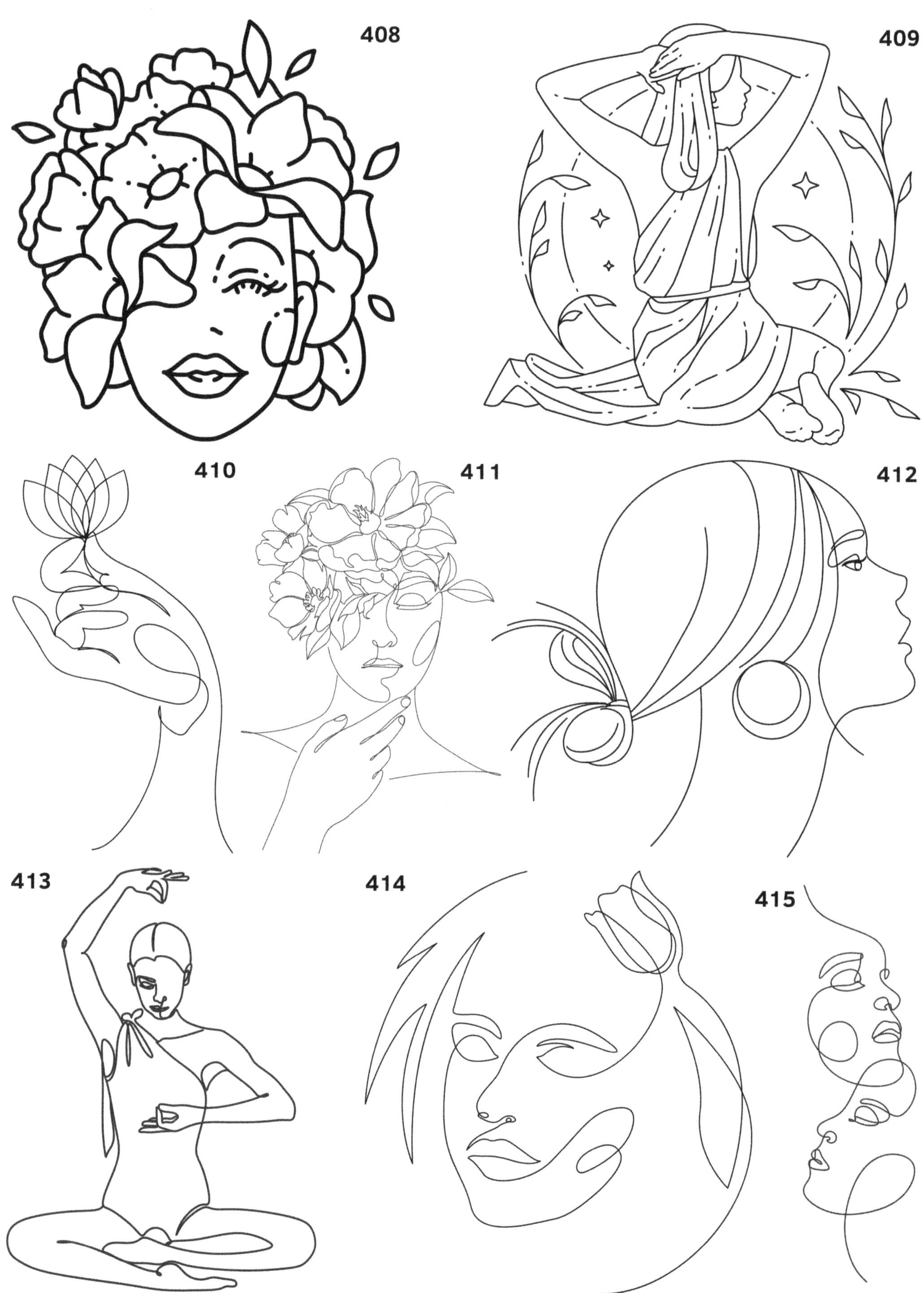

408
409
410
411
412
413
414
415

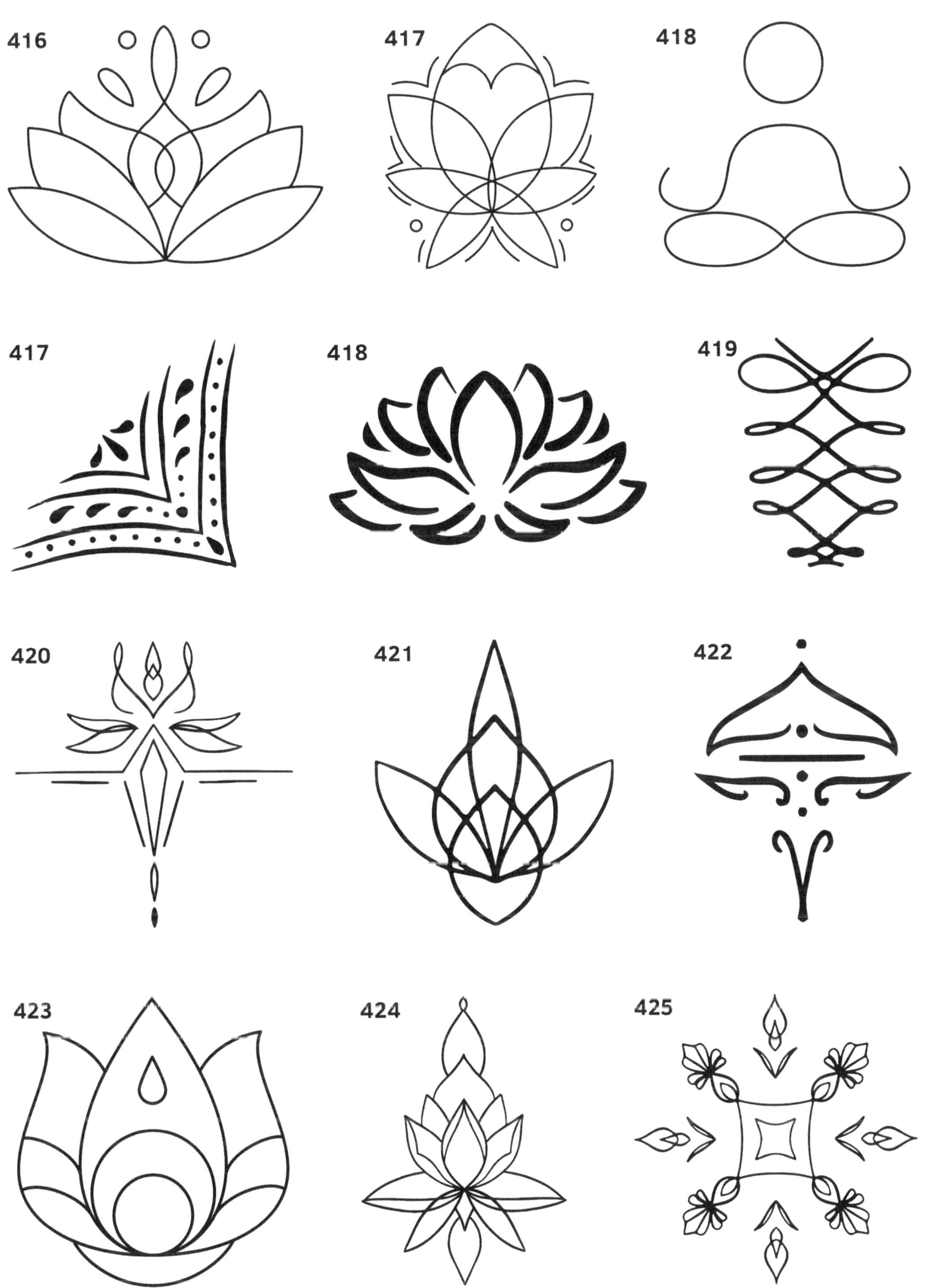

416
417
418
417
418
419
420
421
422
423
424
425

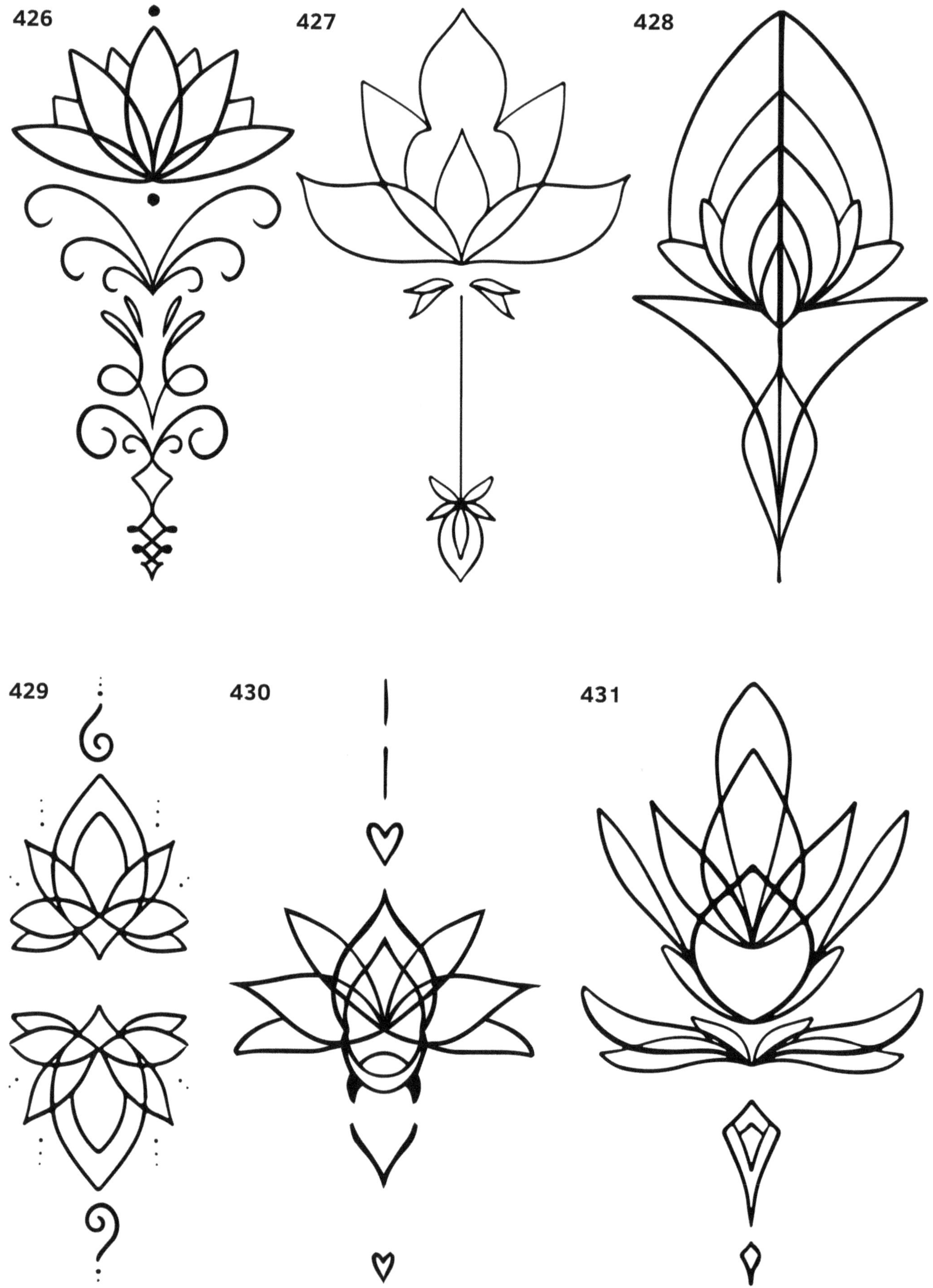
426
427
428
429
430
431

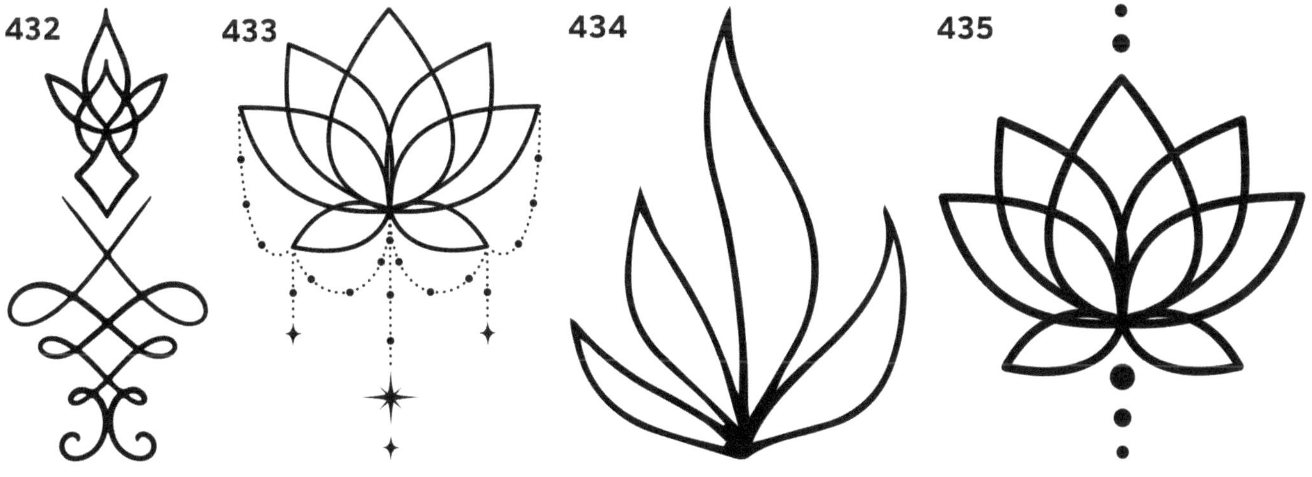

432   433   434   435

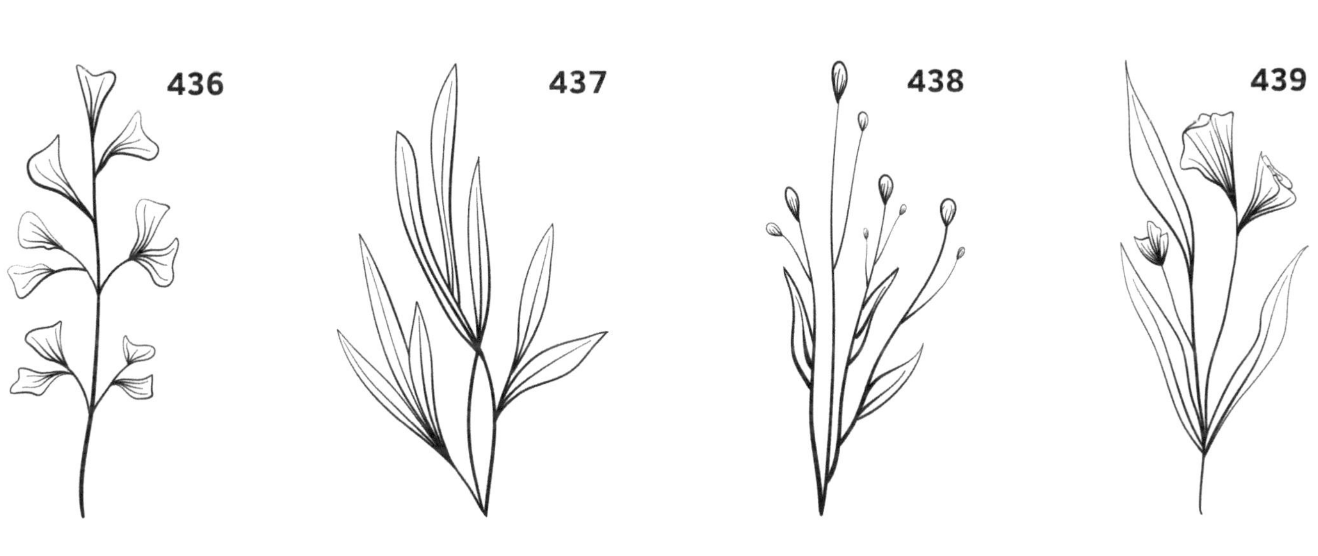

436   437   438   439

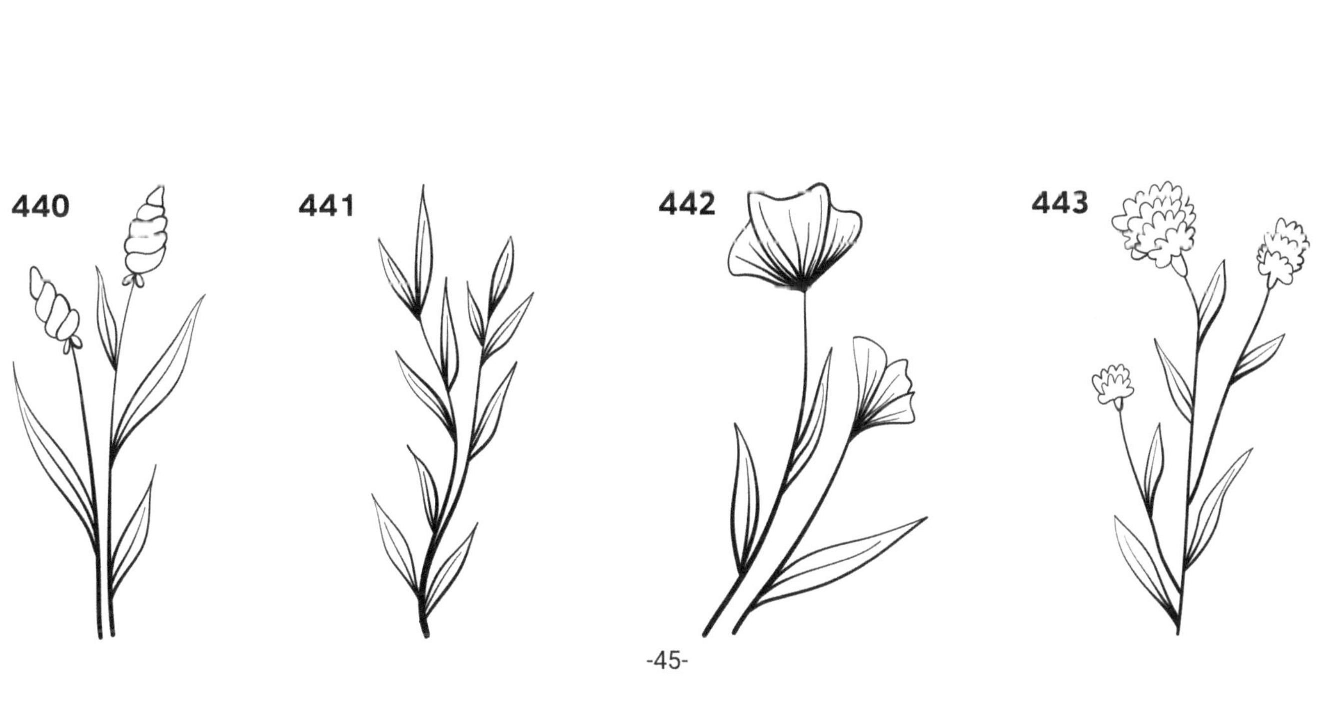

440   441   442   443

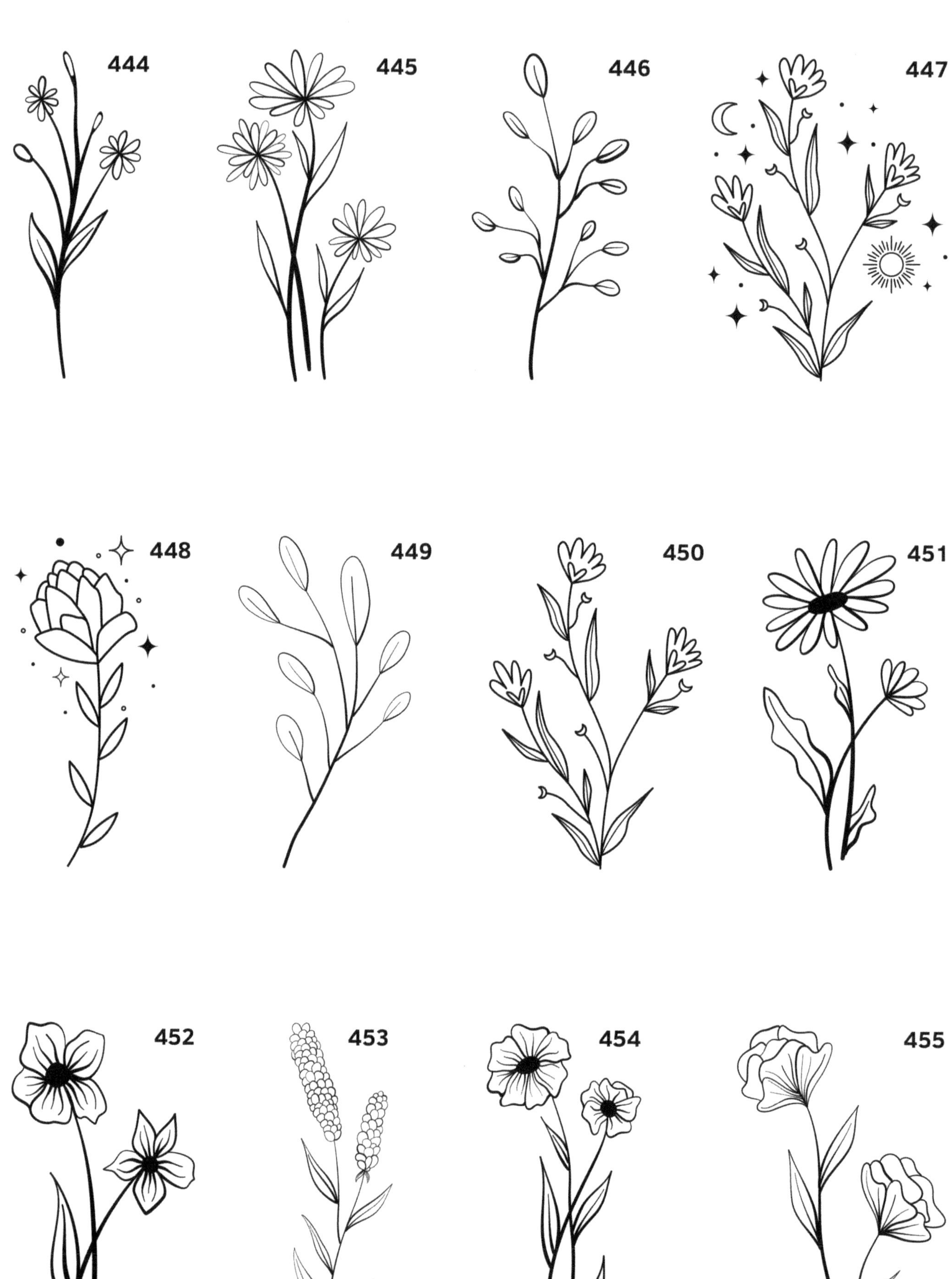

444
445
446
447
448
449
450
451
452
453
454
455

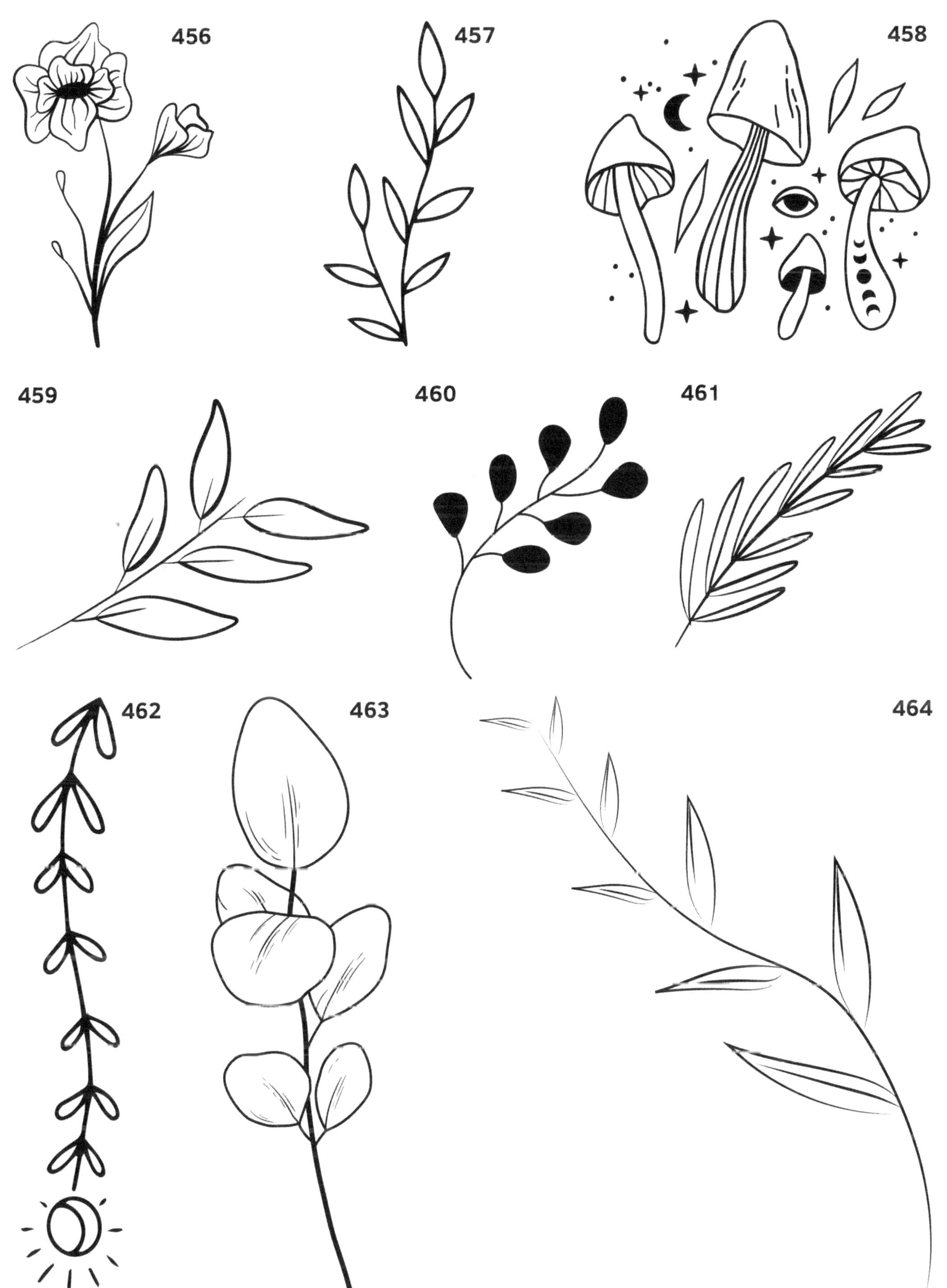

456
457
458
459
460
461
462
463
464

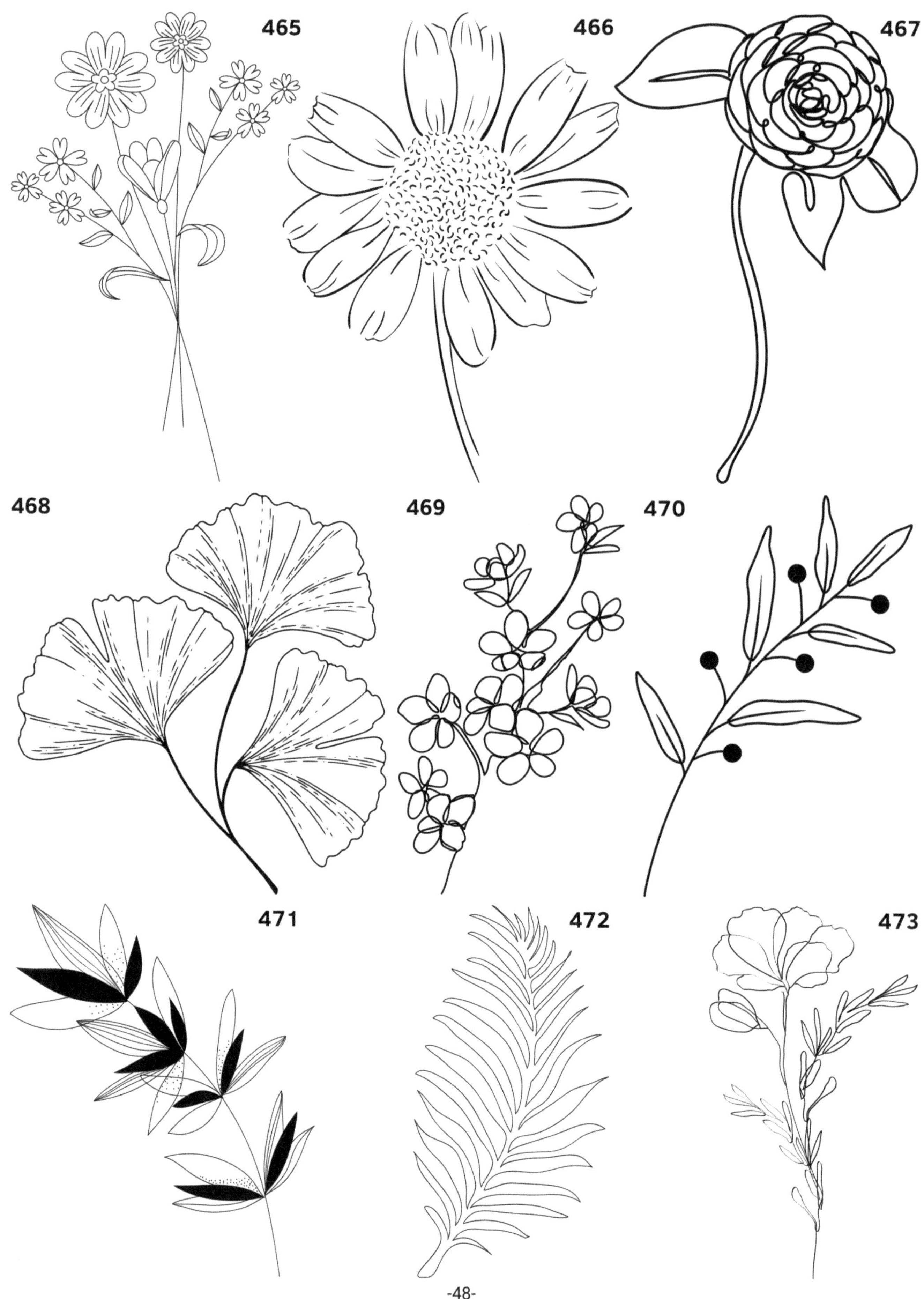

465
466
467
468
469
470
471
472
473

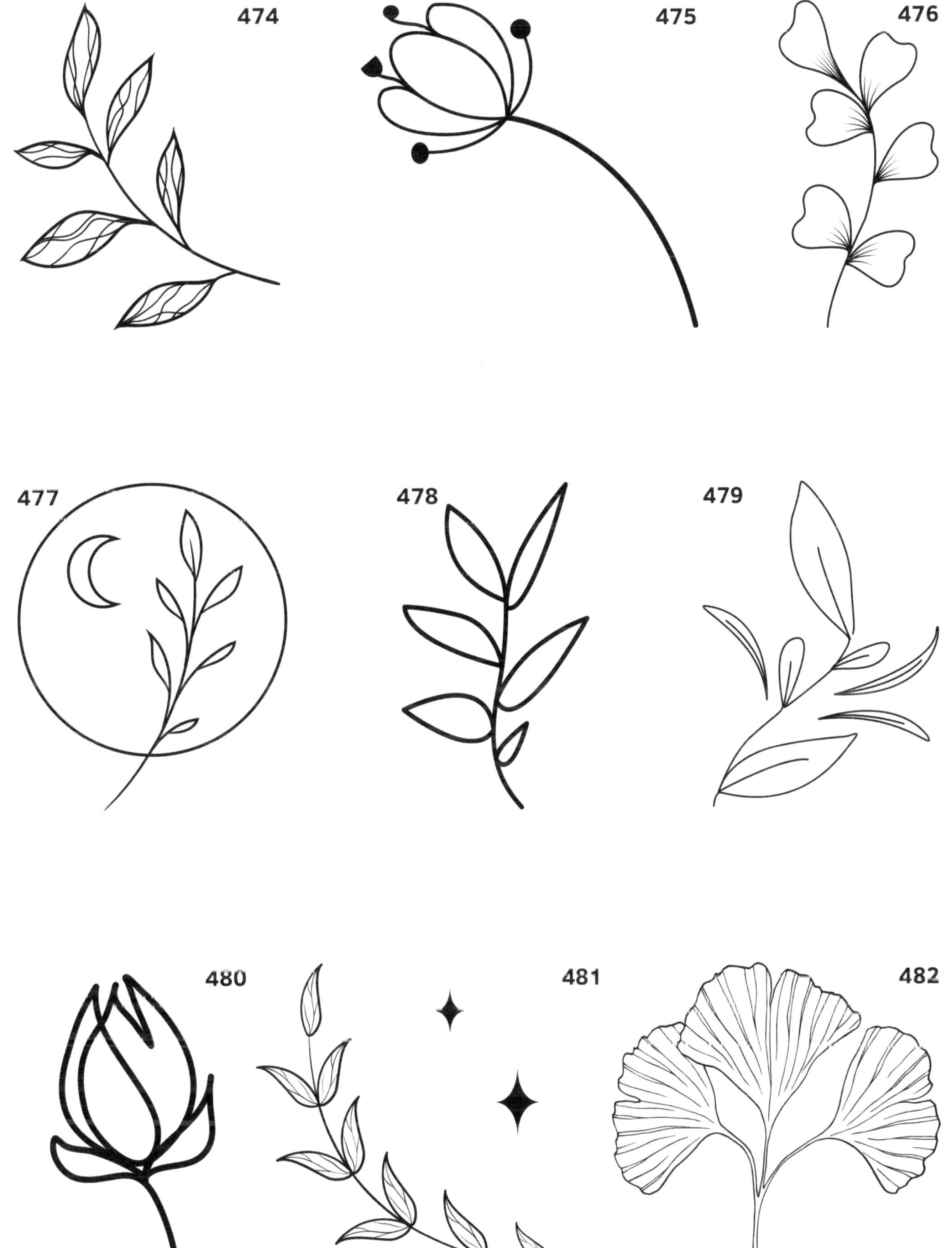

474
475
476
477
478
479
480
481
482

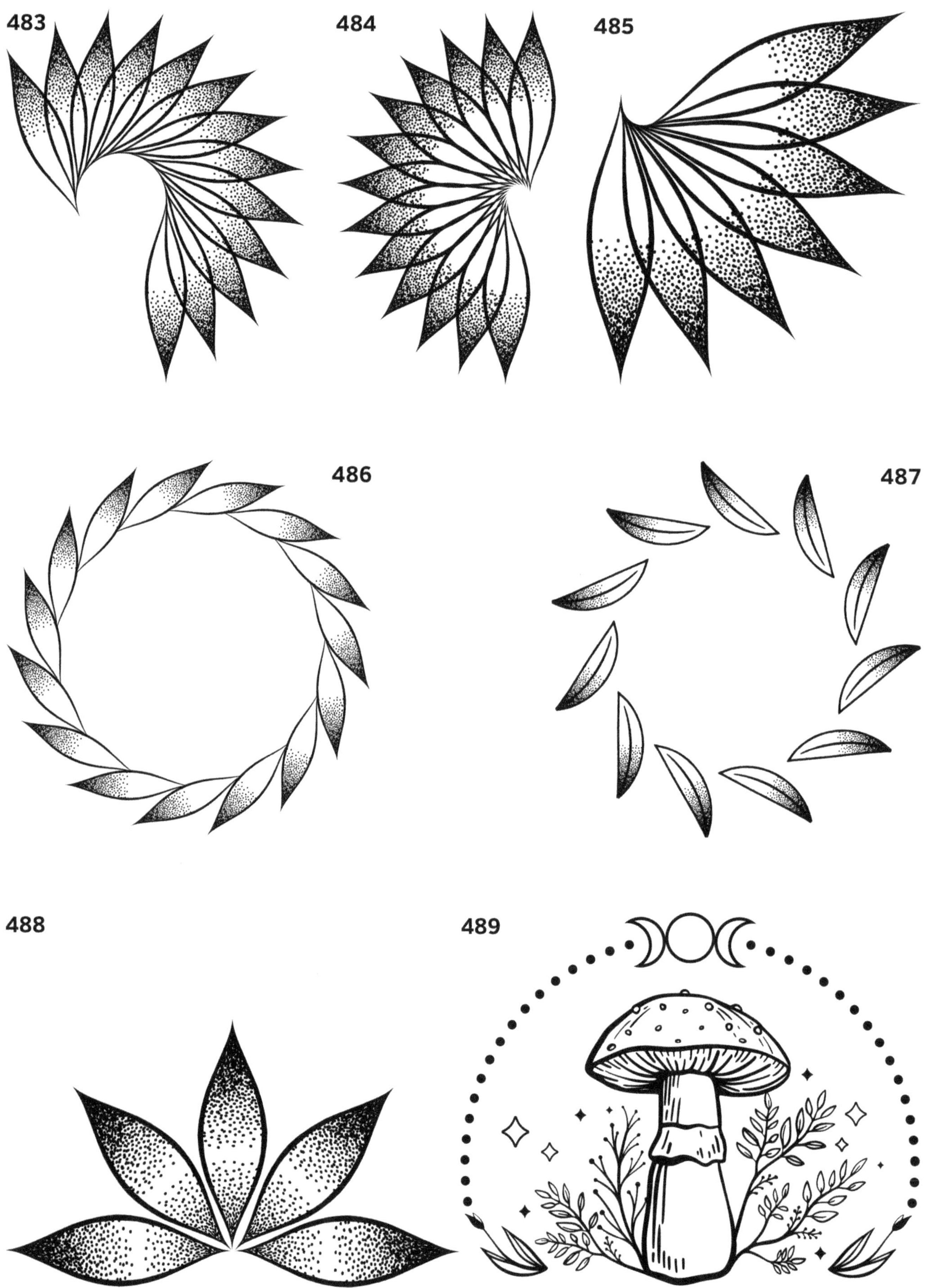

483
484
485
486
487
488
489

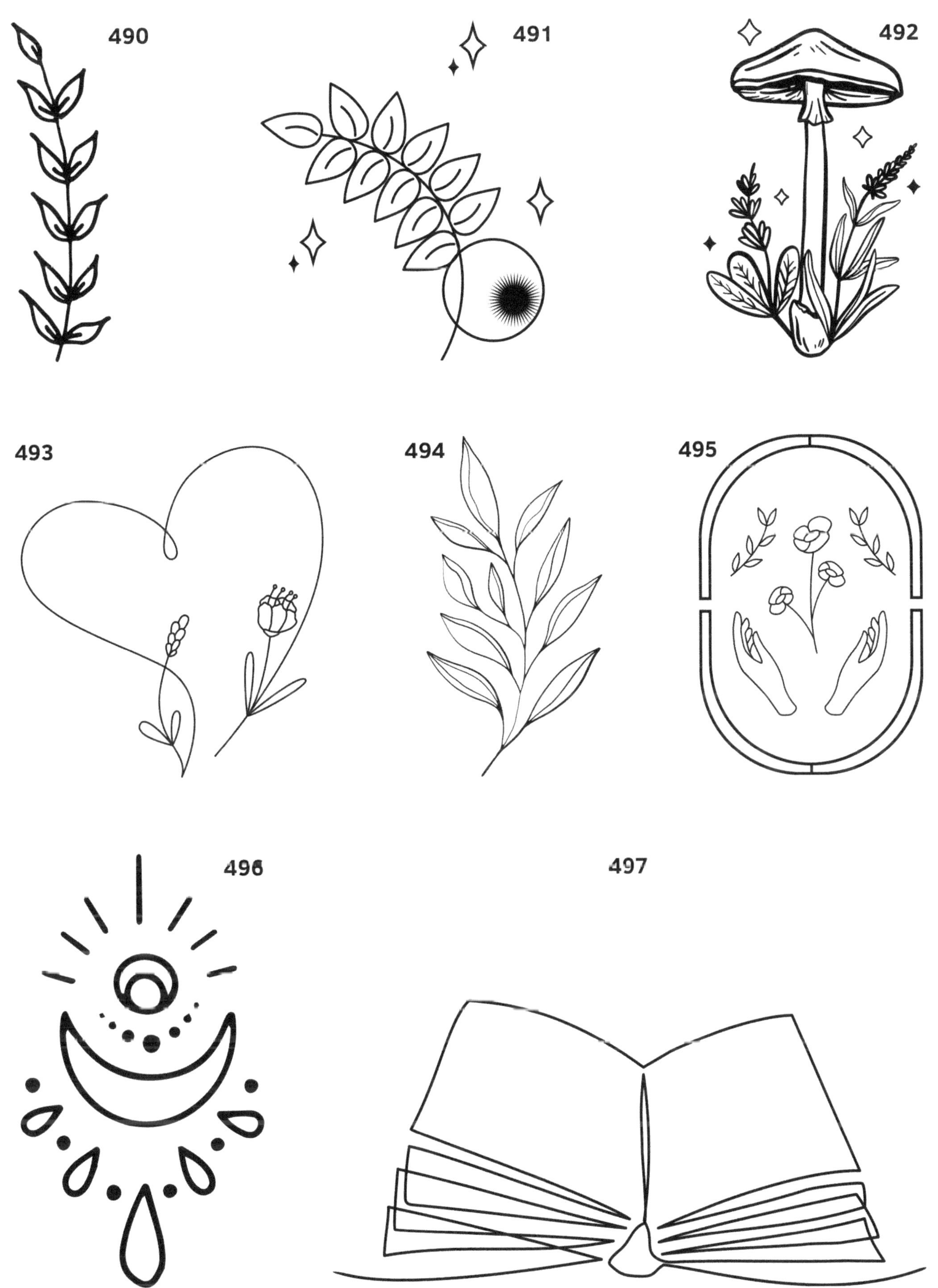

490
491
492
493
494
495
496
497

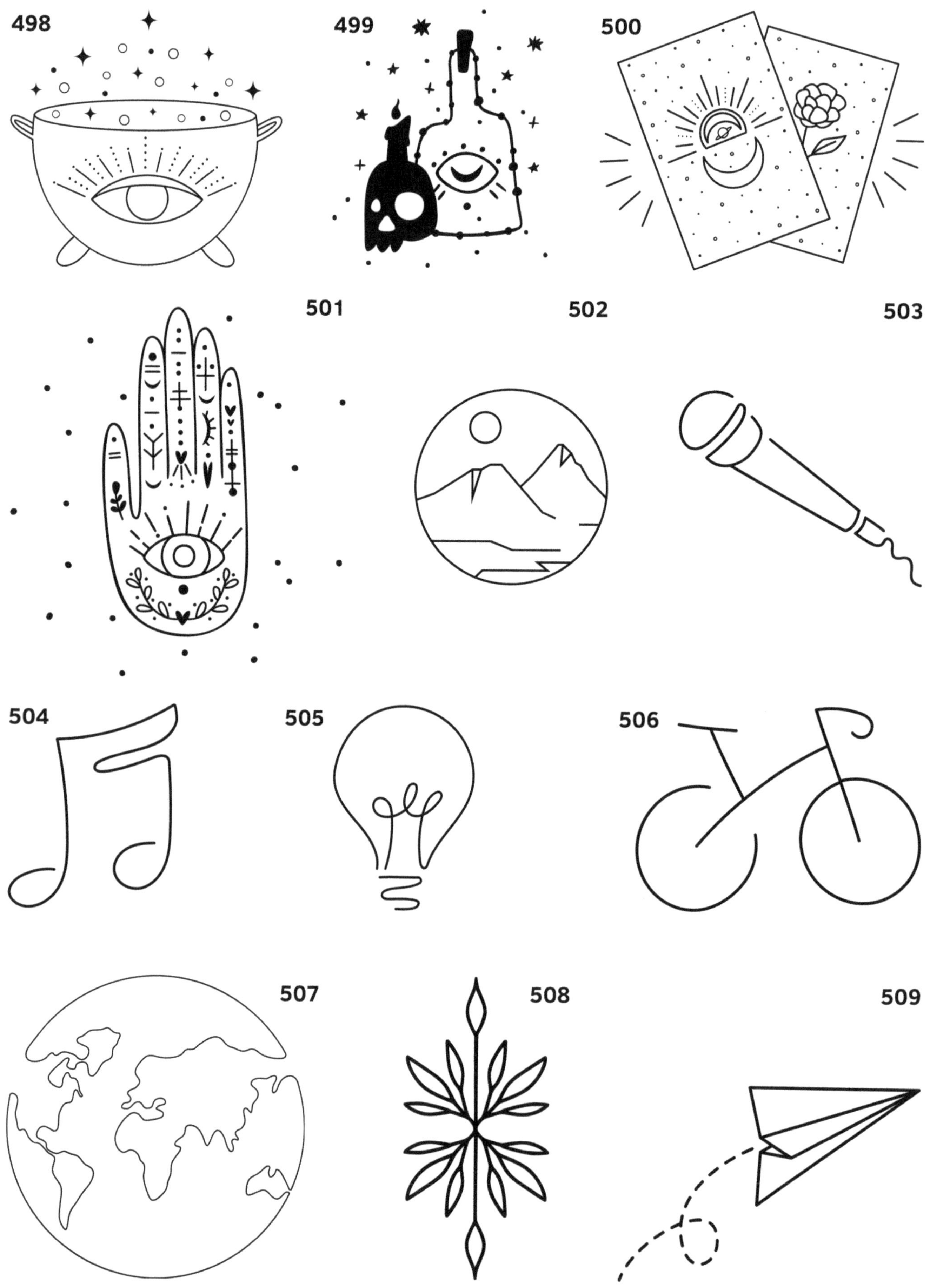

498
499
500
501
502
503
504
505
506
507
508
509

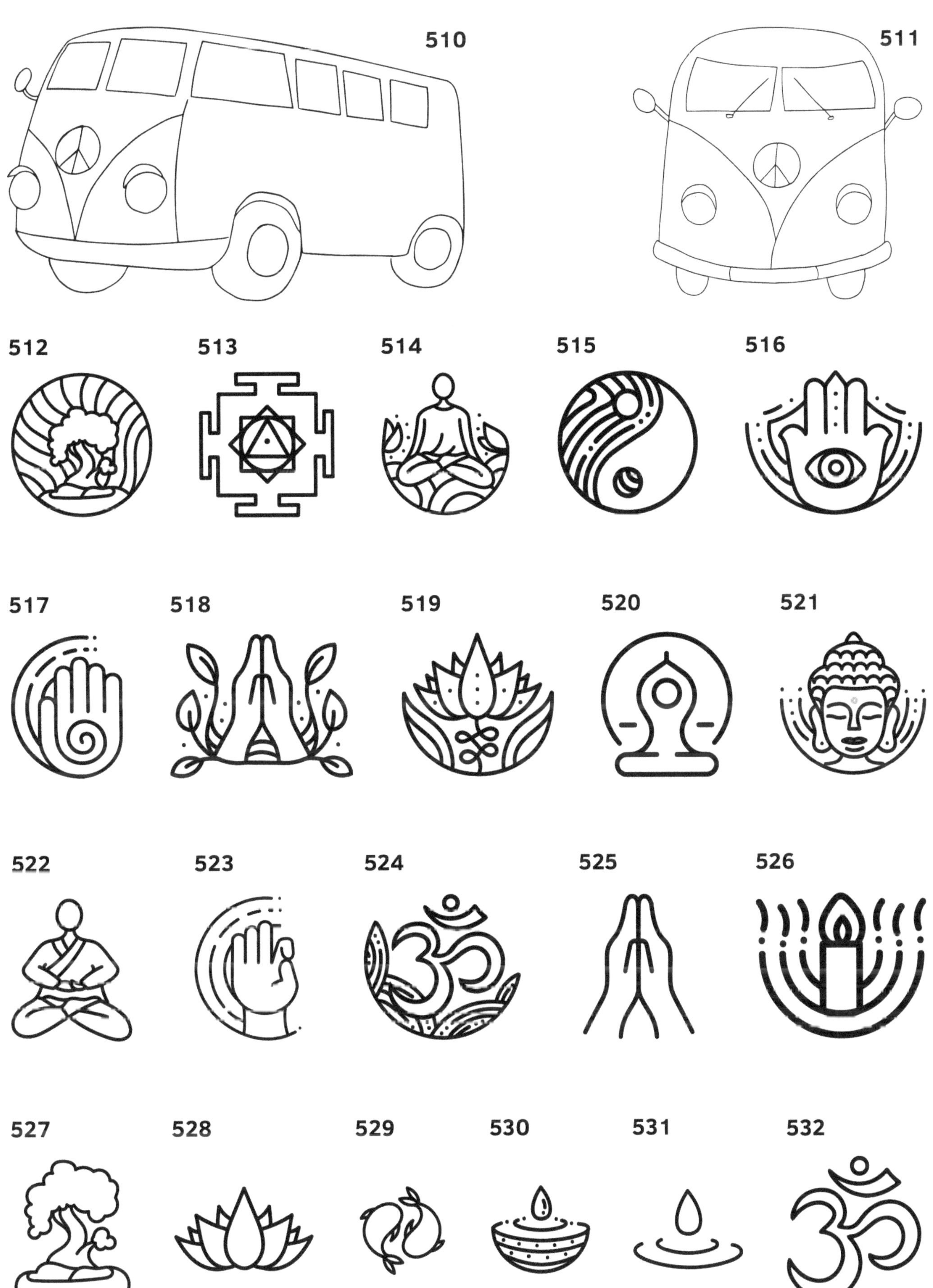

510
511
512
513
514
515
516
517
518
519
520
521
522
523
524
525
526
527
528
529
530
531
532

533 **534** 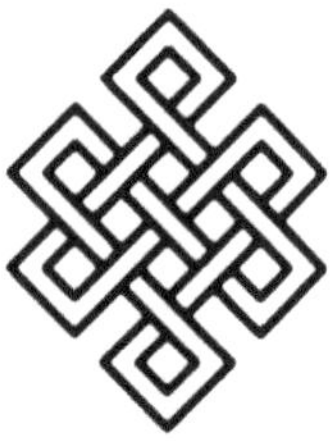 **535** 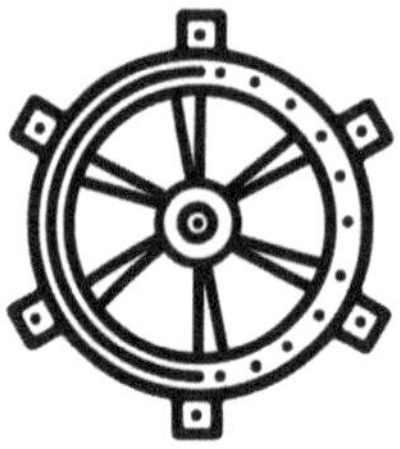 **536** 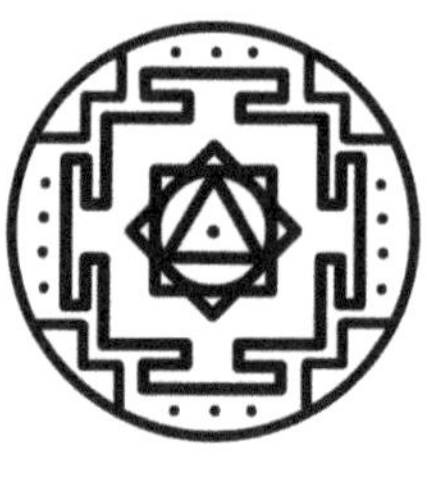 **537**

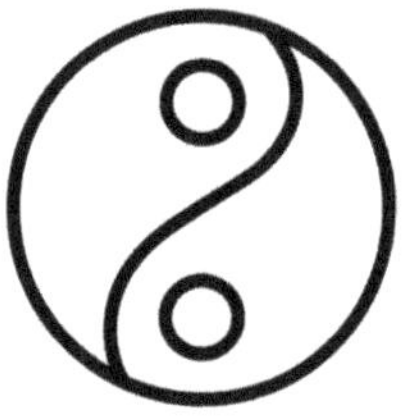

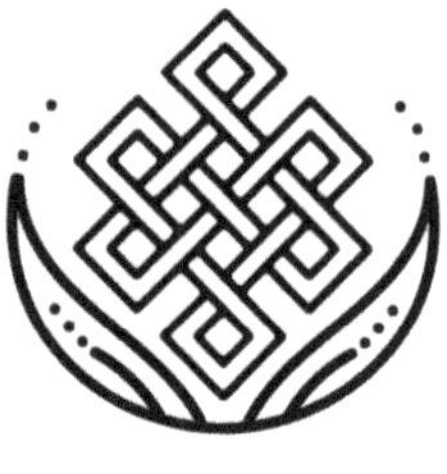

538 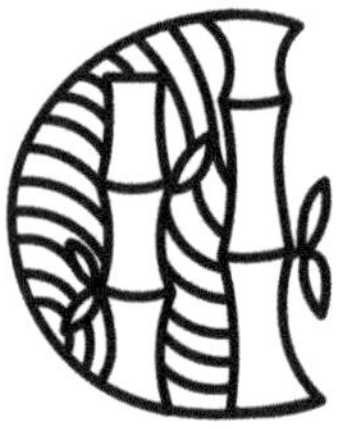 **539** 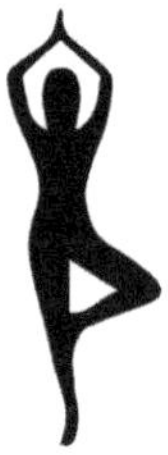 **540** 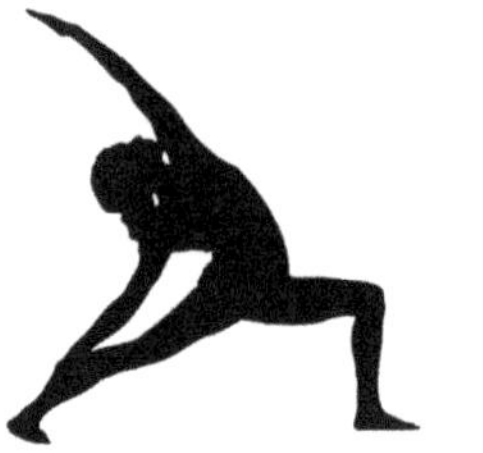 **541** 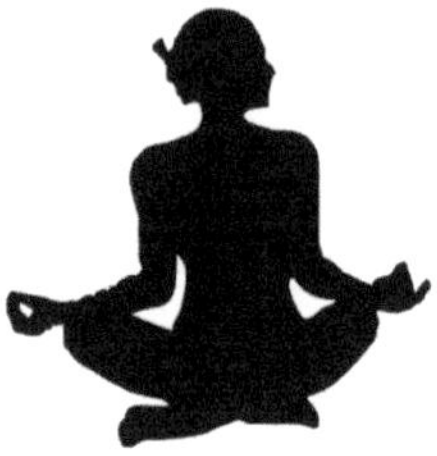 **542**

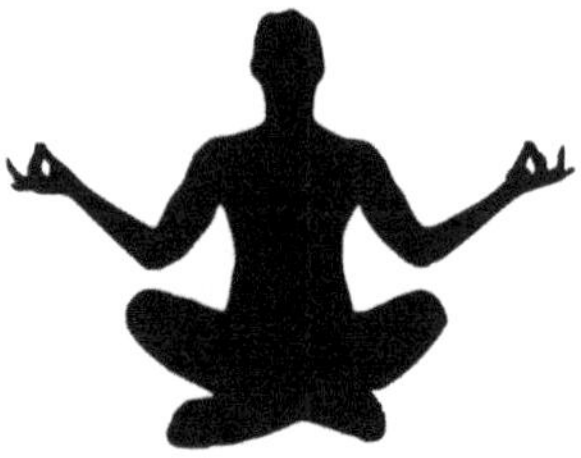

543 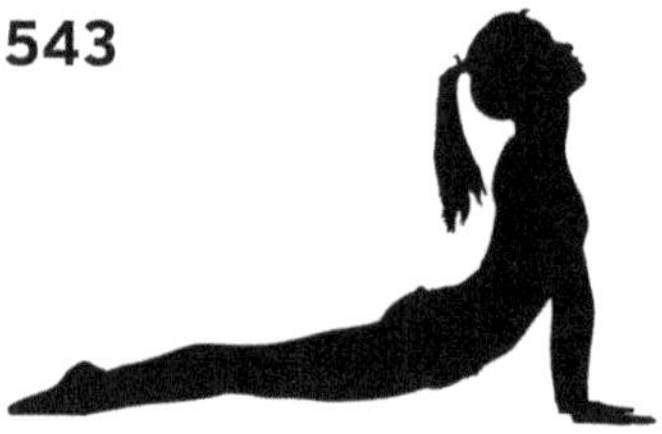 **544** 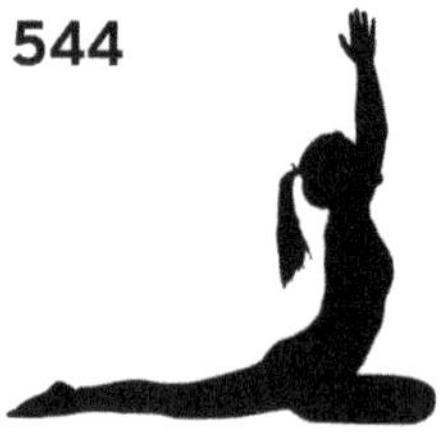 **545** 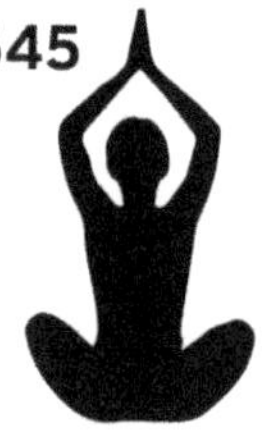 **546** 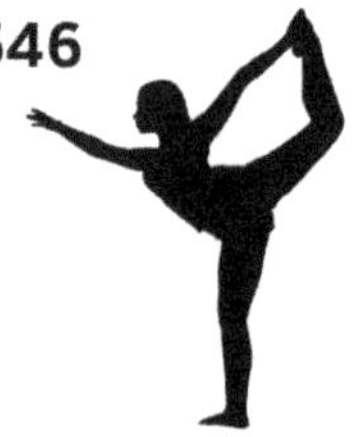 **547**

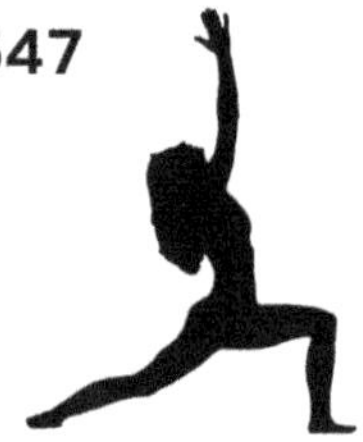

548 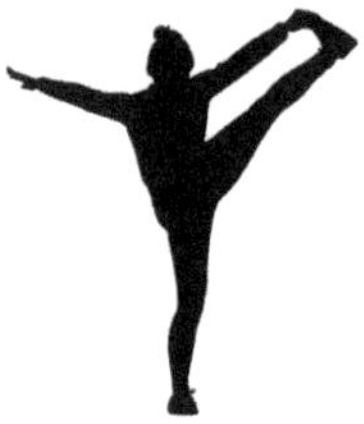 **549** 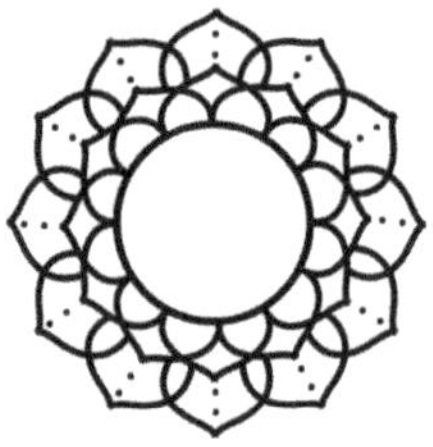 **550**

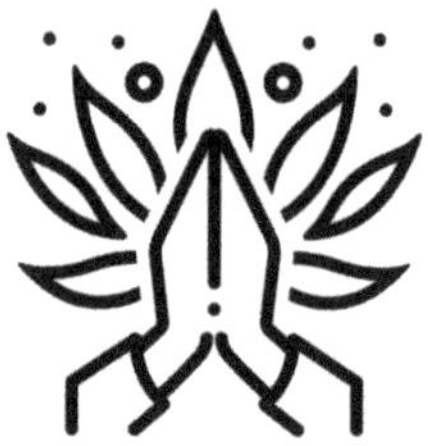

Check these books out:

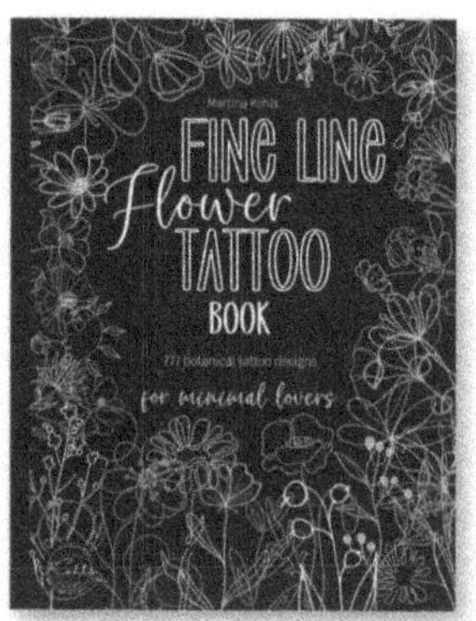

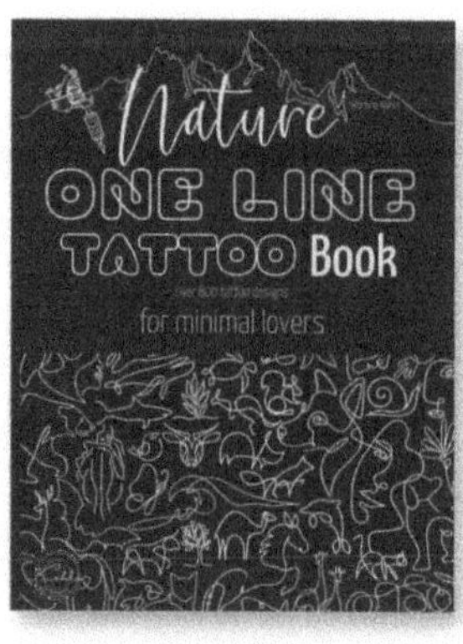

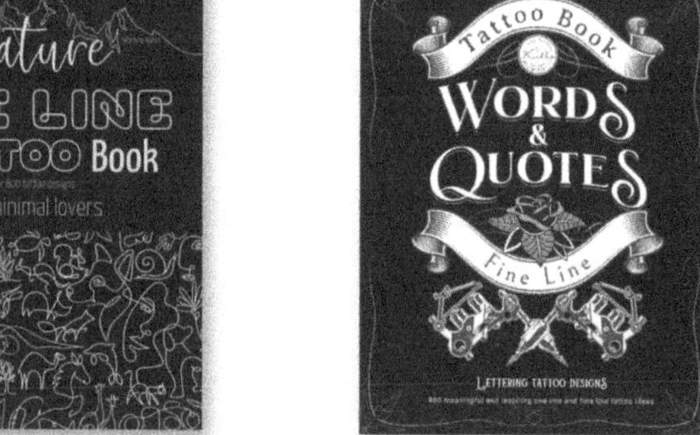

Impressum

Kohls Digiworx
vertreten durch:
Martina Kohls, Lindenstrasse 5, 57648 Bölsberg
Deutschland
ISBN: 978-3-910363-99-1
Independently Published
This book was printed by IngramSpark©